HOMO LUMINOUS
A WORKBOOK FOR CONSCIOUS EVOLUTION

BY

KIARA WINDRIDER

ENDORSEMENTS

HOMO LUMINOUOS

I truly enjoyed this book. It is always the same Truth, but the perspective of Truth the author offers is so very different for me. Like Kiara, I love Sri Aurobindo's reference to the 'sun-eyed children of the marvellous dawn.' This absolutely nvokes the Homo Luminous of the title. Thought provoking in its scale, with his subject deeply and thoroughly researched, this book offers many 'ah ha' moments. I thoroughly recommend that you buy this book, read it, and grow in consciousness.

Michael J. Roads, author of
From Illusion to Enlightenment & Entering the Secret World of Nature

GAIA LUMINOUS

This remarkable book showcases Kiara's extraordinary ability to integrate, summarize and structure a vast range of topics from deeply spiritual teachings to the latest discoveries in science. Kiara brilliantly and eloquently connects the dots, and presents clear and practical solutions for these complex and precarious times. This book will gift you with insights to the past, illuminations in the present and hopes for the future, and will also empower and encourage you to become an active participant in co-creating the New Earth.

Yves Nager, author of Find your Life Purpose

This is a must read for anyone interested in becoming more knowledgeable about the great shift of the ages and planetary awakening that we are in the midst of. I can truly say I have never read a book that is more comprehensive and multi-dimensional. It addresses all levels of this shift, from deeply visionary to supremely practical, from magnetic field collapse and social reconstruction to biological transformation and ascension.

Barry Martin Snyder, co-author of The Luminous Self

As editor of *Gaia Luminous,* I found its content quite illuminating! The beauty and heartfelt accuracy from which Kiara expresses the true condition of humanity and our planet has superseded any expectations I have had from any editing project. Over my many years as a seeker, following a multitude of teachings, I have never come to experience one that expressed the practical wisdom that Kiara seems to be the steward of. I could read his words again and again, to continually discover new threads of information unraveling, revealing and awakening.

Heidi Mason, "Evolutionary Editing"

Gaia Luminous calls each of us to fundamentally alter our human software towards the creation of a better world. This work helps us on our planetary journey into higher consciousness.

Aris Promos Promopoulos, healer

Deep in the human collective psyche is a knowing that the gathering "End Times" chaos heralds a radical transformation for our race and planet. For those who are consciously aware of the challenging implications and seek both cosmic perspectives and spiritual guidance, *Gaia Luminous* is an invaluable resource of scholarly and balanced investigation, combined with profound personal experience.

Simon Peter Fuller, Founder, Wholistic World Vision.

Gaia Luminous helped me through a very dark patch. Kiara's book is masterly in every sense. Combining extraordinary spirituality with a vast array of scientific research, it points to a supramental vision of our cosmic future while acknowledging the horror and corruption holding sway in our present moments. Your thoughts, words and deeds will be shifted forever after reading this.

Margaret More, evolutionary catalyst

Gaia Luminous is a revelation. The first part could pull many of us into fear, but when read with your inner eyes it is a wake-up call, an invitation to understand the big picture. The second part tells a story of hope and provides guidance on how we can take responsibility for our own awakening and the awakening of the planet.

Setara Dolores Piscador, shamanic healer

Your words touched my heart deeply. The book is to be recommended for everybody who is interested in our planet and the well being of our Mother Gaia.

Heidi Verbeke, owner of "Dolphin Heart"

Published by

Kima Global Publishers
50, Clovelly Road
Clovelly
7975
South Africa

ISBN 978-1-928234-22-7

eISBN 978-1-928234-25-8

© Kiara Windrider July 2018

Publisher's Web Site www.kimabooks.com
Author's web site www.kiarawindrider.net

Cover design by: Katja Cloud www.cloud-7-design.de

Graphic designer: Gloria di Simone www.gloriadisimone.tk
assisted by Moira River, hariom999@comcast.net

TABLE OF CONTENTS

Table of Contents

Table of Contents

Homo Luminous

INTRODUCTION

We are here on this Earth to learn how to be fully present. This awareness of presence is easier to experience between incarnations while we are in our causal or subtle bodies. But once we arrive on this planet, entering the density inherent in our collective human matrix, the names and the forms become a substitute for the spontaneous experience of oneness.

Our journey begins with an awareness of who we are, and the realization that this is the same primal awareness that permeates the universe. This is something we already are, so we don't have to go looking for it outside of ourselves. It is time to realize this now, not just on a personal level but on a collective level. We are here on this planet for a collective awakening.

This realization is what some have called enlightenment. In many of our spiritual traditions we are taught to believe that this is a difficult attainment, an ultimate experience that is gained only after long effort and practice. I would like to demonstrate in this book that enlightenment is not as difficult as we are conditioned to believe, and that it is simply about creating bridges between various aspects of human consciousness.

Our current species is conditioned by belief systems that create an abiding sense of separateness. We feel separate from each other, separate from the natural flow of life, separate also from the truth of our own being. This sense of separation is experienced as a duality of consciousness, a sense of being a small and insignificant part of a vast mysterious universe, at the mercy of cosmic events completely outside our own control.

Our suffering comes from feeling separate from the world around us. We wish to control our destiny and cannot. We feel helpless in the face of tumultuous world events. Our inability to trust the river of life plunges us into desperation and fear. We feel we must push ourselves in order to succeed, compete with the world in order to feel valued, or prove ourselves worthy in order to be loved.

Our lives are defined by struggle, bounded by the sense of our own limits. Much as we might like to, we cannot easily imagine a world defined by harmony and joy, in which giving and receiving are part of a spontaneously arising flow that inerrantly seeks the highest good for each of us.

What if the world we experience is not the way it has to be? What if our experience of duality isn't real in itself but rather a way that we have learned to perceive reality? And if we have learned to perceive reality from a state of separation, can we also unlearn this, and begin to shape the world differently?

We speak of different creatures having different levels of consciousness. Humans are more conscious than pigs, pigs are more conscious than plants, plants are more conscious than amoebas, and amoebas are more conscious than a speck of dust. What is the fine line between living and non-living, and is that distinction meaningful anymore?

What if we changed our definition of consciousness? What if we don't have consciousness so much as *are* consciousness. How does that change our relationship with the universe, and with our essential self?

What does it mean to be on a spiritual path? Some traditions speak about matter being inherently dense or stagnant. While acknowledging that we are ultimately beings of spirit and light, there is the assumption that taking incarnation in bodies of matter somehow separates us from the truth of our being, which is spirit. Forgetting that we've never left, we end up walking this earth on a razor's edge, yoked to a wheel of karma that we must do our best to escape from in our journey back to spirit!

The Inka tradition, like many other shamanic cultures around the world, refers to this world as only one of three different worlds, each having its own set of rules and experiences. The world we perceive through eyes of duality, through the lens of subconscious human conditioning, through becoming overly reliant on the rational mind and physical senses, is referred to as the middle world. It is not the only world that can be experienced in our physical bodies, however.

There are worlds that can be experienced that lie outside the scope of the rational mind. Shamans refer to these as the upper worlds and the lower worlds. They are not less real than the middle world, but it requires that we learn to use different structures of the mind in order to experience them. Ultimately, it is about living multi-dimensionally, learning to experience reality through the simultaneous awareness of all these aspects of the mind.

As we learn to perceive reality differently, reality changes to match our perceptions. Ultimately we learn that the world we have been conditioned to believe as real is a relative illusion. As we learn to see differently we discover that we have power to change the world in ways we never imagined.

I am reminded of the movie, *The Matrix*, where Morpheus offers Neo a choice between the blue pill and the red pill. I believe that the blue pill represents the reality bounded by the middle world, mediated by the rational mind, and conditioned by our collective experience of duality, a world that has proved itself to be an asylum for the insane, a world increasingly heading towards its own inevitable demise. We do not have much time left as a species if we choose to remain trapped within this matrix.

But what if we took the red pill? Is it possible to exit this matrix? The answer to that is a resounding YES. This book is about taking the red pill, and offers a blueprint for multi-dimensional consciousness, weaving together teachings and practices from traditions that have succeeded in hacking our current matrix of reality. Ultimately it is a vision of a new species emerging on this Earth, which, like Neo, has learned to see past the illusion and recognize that we are creators in this great living universe, and not simply victims.

There are several sources of insight that I weave together in this book. First, there are the shamanic traditions, which are about learning to see differently. I will specifically focus on the *Q'ero Inka* tradition here, which in my own experience offers uniquely simple and powerful practices for opening doorways between the worlds.

I also share practices from the *Ilahinoor* tradition birthed in Turkey, designed to open doorways between various structures of the mind, and to anchor galactic frequencies of light into the cells of our physical bodies.

The *Advaita* traditions of India offer a glimpse into who we are, not simply as a philosophy to nourish the mind but also as a way of empowering ourselves as creators of destiny. We are both divine and human, creator and creation, and the distinction between them melts away as we understand these truths.

I also share the supramental vision of Sri Aurobindo and the Mother, an integral yoga that allows us to birth together an entirely new species of humanity that is no longer bounded by separation and duality, but is genetically programmed to live in states of cosmic awareness and unity.

And finally, I summarize insights from neuroscience, evolutionary biology, astrophysics, plasma cosmology and systems theory, which provide clues for what our collective evolution might look like.

This book, *Homo Luminous,* is a companion to *Gaia Luminous.* While Gaia Luminous provides a road map to understanding and creating the New Earth, *Homo Luminous* is an eminently practical guide for building the energy structures within our bodies for manifesting our latent multi-dimensional destiny as *divine humans.*

In order to directly experience some of the practices here, please watch the following recording of a workshop offered in Taos, New Mexico in September 2015:

https://youtu.be/3PdEOqTIkhs.

PART I

THE MAP

Homo Luminous

I see a garden beyond the flames
To enter I must burn away
Everything I have ever identified with
All the stories I have ever told
Everyone I have ever known or loved
All ideas of separation and loss
Even my yearnings for union
I must enter empty handed
Expecting nothing
Offering everything I am in return
Such a small price to pay
For the garden of my soul!

Kiara Windrider

CHAPTER 1
INKA COSMOVISION

I have always been interested in the shamanic traditions. My first teacher in this mysterious world of expanded perception was Carlos Castaneda. Along with an entire generation of seekers in the Sixties, I found myself fascinated by Castaneda's books featuring the Yaqui shaman, Don Juan Matus, who takes him on a *journey of power* that cracks open his perception of reality forever. He introduces him to the *nagual,* an entirely different order of reality, where entire worlds can be constructed and deconstructed based on learning to *see* differently.

The spiritual path is about learning to see rightly, and to see rightly we must engage the heart. "For me there is only the traveling on paths that have heart," says Don Juan. "There I travel, and the only worthwhile challenge is to traverse its full length. And there I travel, looking, looking breathlessly".

During my college years I immersed myself in the ceremonial world of the Lakota people, seeking to walk this *path with heart,* to connect with the depth and power of a tradition that acknowledges the *one spirit that moves through all things.* Through sweat lodges and occasional vision quests I learned to access doorways between the worlds, and touch a magical web of life existing beneath the world of ordinary perception.

Later, as I undertook a program in transpersonal psychology, I began to understand how the body and spirit were not separate from each other, as many spiritual traditions erroneously taught. They only appeared to be separate from a conditioned perception of the mind, and as I learned to access expanded states of mind and consciousness, the illusion of separation quickly faded away.

Although I was willing to explore the role of plant medicines such as mescaline, peyote and ayahuasca in accessing non-ordinary states of consciousness, I eventually realized that if I wished to be an agent of change in the ordinary world, I would also need to liberate the full power of the conscious mind, de-conditioning this lens of perception so that the conscious mind could easily access and integrate subconscious and superconscious perceptions of reality.

I learned to work with breath, rhythm and movement as a way of bridging between the worlds. I learned different forms of healing. I began to work with people using the tools and perspectives of transpersonal psychology, which recognizes the unity of body mind and spirit as a means for understanding as well as influencing reality.

And then later in my life I met my own Don Juan, in the form of Don Juan Nunez del Prado, a Peruvian anthropologist and *paqo*, who presented in his teachings and initiations a beautiful cosmovision based on ancient Andean traditions. While sharing much in common with other shamanic traditions around the world, these teachings also offered perspectives and practices that were unique and powerful.

The Inka tradition goes back thousands of years to earlier cycles of civilization. Much of this ancient Inka knowledge has been hidden since the Spanish conquest of the 16th century, except in the hands of the few traditional communities in the high mountains who preserved their culture and traditions.

The Q'ero Indians of Peru, the Kogis of Colombia, the Kawayas in Bolivia, and the Otabalos of Ecuador were some of these survivors. They still exist in their hidden mountain villages, still carrying the teachings of their ancestors. In many cases these teachings are being made available once more as we prepare for the collective transition from one world age to the next.

I would like to summarize here some of this cosmovision so we can sense their relevance and power in the culture of uncertainty and chaos that characterizes the modern age. Later in the book, I will be presenting some of these teachings as guided meditations.

The Inkas, like many indigenous people around the world, experience the universe as a living presence. In the *Quechua* language, this living presence that permeates the universe is known as *kausay pacha*. They don't make a distinction between things and beings. Everything has a quality of life and carries *kausay*, or life energy, whether stars, mountains, earthworms, a speck of dust or a human being.

Western cosmovision distinguishes between living and non-living, and places human at the top of a hierarchy of value. This has led us to perceive existence as survival of the fittest, rather than an invitation to seek beauty and balance in a living web of life. We define the world from a perspective of scarcity and so feel the need to conquer. The Inka cosmovision is the opposite. Nature gives abundantly and freely, and our responsibility is to give back. Abundance is never possible at the expense of anybody else.

There is a constant flow of energy that connects all things in the universe, which they refer to as *sami*. *Sami* moves continuously in a beautiful dance of creation, based in the principle of *ayni*, or reciprocity. This is an important principle, as we will examine later. Humans who do not honor ayni block the flow of *sami*, and hence develop a heavy energy, or *hucha*, which veils us from a true perception of reality.

Hucha often takes the form of fear, where we dare not trust the natural flow of life, and therefore learn to resist it, creating a sense of separation within our psyche. Our lack of under-standing also leads to attachments and addictions, which create suffering. Or we tend to accumulate things, whereas our true wealth is in letting go.

All this closes down the doorways between the worlds and keeps us stuck in the colorless void of conditioned reality. Thus, our journey of remembrance is about learning to attune to the living forces all around us, and release the heavy energies that keep us trapped in separation, fear and limitation.

Kausay is like a mountain stream, they explain. When it is flowing it is fresh and clear. When it becomes blocked the water stagnates. Humans have the unique capacity in creation to block the flow, to create hucha. But unblock the flow, and soon the water will be clean again.

As Juan Nunez and his son Ivan led us through some of these teachings and initiations, I could feel the very clear presence of the Inka lineage that stood behind them, extending back through their own teachers, and rooted in the understanding that we all carry the seeds of divinity within us, which is what the word *Inka* essentially means.

The *quechua* word used to describe an Andean priest is *paqo*, which includes within its definition both shaman and mystic. A *shaman* is one who traditionally seeks power in order to heal or access needed information. A *mystic* is one who seeks wisdom, a direct understanding of the essential nature of the cosmos. The Inka path embraces both, and provides simple tools where each of us can become a *paqo*.

Our thoughts, concepts and perceptions are interpretations of reality, not reality itself. The idea that we are separate entities moving through time is a product of the rational mind, and only has meaning in the middle world, or the *kai pacha*. The goal of a paqo is to break out of the matrix of the rational mind, and to directly experience the inter-connectedness of all things.

As *paqos*, we each have the privileged position of existing simultaneously in all three worlds of creation, the *hanaq pacha* or heavenly realms, the *kai pacha* or earthly realms, and the *ukhu pacha*, the underworld of subconscious archetypes which drive our evolution. The Inka practices assist in opening the doorways between these worlds so we can walk between them at all times.

We are constantly supported in this by Father Cosmos above (*Wiracocha*), and Mother Cosmos below (*Pachamama*). They represent electrical and magnetic streams of light that permeate the universe. All matter is a manifestation of Pachamama, just as all spirit is a manifestation of Wiracocha.

The Inka practices we were taught are rooted in this understanding of the cosmos, and represent a path of freedom as we learn to reconnect with the *inka muju,* or seed of enlightenment, that lies dormant within us. As we move through these current times of *pachakuti,* or upheaval, these teachings and practices can help forge a path towards the new human species that is emerging in the world now.

There is the Andean prophecy about the *taripay pacharuna, the age of meeting ourselves again.* The Hopi people in North America have a similar saying, *We are the ones we have been waiting for.* The condor and the eagle are meeting now, and a new world is dreaming itself awake!

CHAPTER 2
ILAHINOOR

What does this new world look like? What are the evolutionary forces at work? What are the mechanisms that shape our journey of awakening, not just in our personal lives but as a collective human species?

Some time ago, as I describe more fully in *Gaia Luminous*, I became aware of galactic and planetary cycles that shape the evolution of all life on our planet. I also became aware that this evolution is not separate from our inner perceptions and intentions, and that we have a co-creative role in birthing a new world age.

We are creators as well as creation, spirit as well as matter, a neurological bridge between heaven and earth. We are a species that has evolved to a point where we can consciously join with the power of sky and earth, and play a role in new biological evolution. Will we waste the gift we are given in dangerous egoic games of artificial intelligence or mindless destruction, or will we align ourselves with the larger purpose that seeks to move through us and shape a new living earth?

Ilahinoor refers to a stream of light that has its own intelligence and evolutionary purpose. As I share in my book, *Ilahinoor:*

Awakening the Divine Human, it literally means *divine light*, and refers to a transmission of galactic frequencies that transcends any distinction between ordinary perceptions of darkness and light.

Translated in Inka terms, it refers to a quality of *sami* which has the very specific function of integrating the nervous system and shaping our biology to evolve toward a new human species.

On a physical level it represents an incoming wave of cosmic rays and gamma rays moving towards our solar system from the galactic center. On a spiritual level it represents the deeper embodiment of a vast universal intelligence, interacting within bodies of matter to awaken new genetic pathways where we learn to consciously step into the next phase of human and planetary evolution.

These incoming waves are getting stronger as we get close to the actual moment of shift, the *taripay pacharuna.* There is a Mayan prophecy about *three days of darkness*, a prelude to this moment of birth. This prophecy seems to be tied in to a process known as the *magnetic reversal,* a recurring and predictable cycle that governs the mechanics of evolution.

Scientists tell us that we are in the final phases of the magnetic reversal now, which refers to a reversal of the earth's magnetic poles, north becoming south and south becoming north. While the initial phase of this reversal process is typically gradual, it rapidly becomes exponential, with the final phase of collapse and reversal taking only two or three days.

The term, *three days of darkness,* thus refers to this final phase of reversal. We are deep into the process already. The final phase seems to be synchronized with incoming galactic superwaves and corresponding solar cycles, which typically produce significant amounts of flaring and other solar activity, generating magnetic ring currents around the earth, leading to the eventual collapse and reversal of the planetary magnetic field.

Some researchers have investigated cycles of magnetic reversal in the past and equated them with evolutionary leaps, indicating a loss of species as well as the creation of new species, precisely during these times of magnetic reversal. Other researchers point to these times of reversal as opportunities for tremendous shifts of consciousness, perhaps due to the fact that the weakening of magnetic fields also reflects the loss of egoic identity in the matrix of duality.

The *three days of darkness* can be likened to the cocooning phase of a caterpillar's journey. As biological controls weaken and old identities dissolve, a process of metamorphosis takes place culminating in the birth of what appears to be an entirely different life form, the butterfly. This process of metamorphosis is assisted by the bombardment of incoming solar and cosmic radiation during this final phase of collapse and reversal. As the magnetopause around the earth weakens, this cosmic radioactivity works with the consciousness of the earth to actively create entirely new species.

Ilahinoor represents a cosmic field of intelligence that is capable of interacting with the intelligence of Gaia, the living earth. From a systems perspective, humans represent the nervous system of Gaia. As we open to these cosmic evolutionary frequencies, we become a bridge between heaven and earth through which a new cycle of evolution can be initiated.

There are specific ways we can begin to anchor these frequencies into and through our bodies, which some of us were guided to develop, starting about ten years ago when I lived in Turkey. Much of this has to do with how the brain functions, and the possibility of linking these functions of the brain so that the conscious levels of the mind can work more harmoniously with subconscious and superconscious levels of the mind. We will describe and utilize these practices in the following section of this book.

CHAPTER 3
THE ADVAITA TRADITION

Underlying our evolutionary journey is an assumption that there is a field of Intelligence within the universe that is directing the process, an intelligence which permeates all things and connects all things. As the Inka *paqos* understood, the universe is a living energy system, each part being in constant communication with every other part. This is an understanding that has not only been intuited in ancient traditions of the world, but is now also being acknowledged in a new branch of science known as *plasma cosmology*, or *the electric universe theory*.

This view of the universe theorizes that the universe is held together through electrical forces rather than gravitational forces. Electrical fields link fields of plasma across vast distances, such that any event that takes place in any corner of the universe instantly affects everything else everywhere else. It is as if the universe were an immense spider web made of interconnected filaments, with a giant invisible spider capable of instantly sensing and responding to every perturbation in the field. Matter arises where these filaments come together to form magnetic nodes. Since electricity and magnetism are interconnected, energy and matter are constantly weaving back and forth through one inter-connected web of life.

There is a brilliant metaphor in the ancient Hindu tradition that beautifully describes this. It is said that the universe is like an infinite string of pearls, with each pearl reflecting every other pearl, each pearl containing every other pearl, and each pearl experiencing every other pearl. This understanding of the universe befuddles the rational mind, but makes absolute sense from a *shamanic* or *advaita* perspective.

Advaita, in the ancient Hindu tradition, means *not two*. It is a road map for understanding our place in the universe from this holographic perspective. Simply stated, it asserts that there is only one consciousness that moves through all things, which is something we have already begun to grasp from the shamanic worldview. But it goes further, and says that in the deepest place of being, who I am IS this undivided consciousness, a consciousness that has existed eternally beyond the confines of time space and creation, but also permeates all of time, space and creation.

This is the ultimate truth, and everything else is relative illusion. Properly understood it means that the self I have identified with through most of my life is a relative illusion, and that I can learn to shift my sense of identity from the personal ego to this undivided core consciousness which permeates all things, and find my true identity there. It means also, of course, that the Self that moves through me is the same Self that moves through you, that the entire universe is a single movement of life. We are holographically connected as a single living organism.

The old paradigm of science tells us that the physical universe was somehow created in a single instant known as the Big Bang, and that in the course of time the first simple elements of matter clumped together to create amino acids which gave birth to life. Life forms eventually developed a mind, and then mind evolved the ability to experience consciousness. Consciousness is somehow associated with the brain's ability to think.

The *advaita* philosophy turns this upside down. First exists Consciousness, it asserts, and consciousness permeates all things, simply because consciousness is existence, and everything that exists is conscious. The field of Consciousness then extends itself to create Mind, which organizes itself to create Life and Matter. All things are connected because it is the one undivided consciousness that moves through all things.

The sense of separation we experience with our senses (including the rational mind) only appears to be real due to the imposition of a creative principle known as *maya,* which operates in the realm of the *kai pacha,* or middle world. The world out there only appears to have a physical reality because of *maya.* It is this principle of maya that generates the illusion of time and space, and therefore of a material reality permeating time and space.

Just because it is an illusion doesn't make it bad. A movie playing in the theater is an illusion, but can affect us deeply in a number of ways. We don't need to settle for someone else's version of a horror movie. We can choose the kind of movie we want to watch, just as we can choose the movie playing across the screen of our minds.

Our experience of the physical world is a function of the rational mind, refined and developed over millions of years of biological evolution. However, as we learn to shift our perceptions beyond the limits of the rational mind we discover a deeper truth. We are not only these precious human person-alities existing within bodies of matter, but also the cons-ciousness eternally self-existing beyond time, space and matter. We are advaita, not two.

Perhaps the concept that has done most to create a wedge between the physical world and the spirit world is the Big Bang, the idea that the universe was created in a moment of time, that the universe has an age, and that time has been unfolding in a linear direction ever since then. This assumption negates the continuity between spiritual consciousness and material consciousness. How does time evolve from the timeless, or form evolve from the formless?

A number of scientists are now questioning whether the Big Bang actually happened, asserting instead that the universe is in a process of continuous creation and dissolution. Instead of a single big bang that created the universe, we blink in and out of existence, fluctuating between time and timelessness, form and formlessness, trillions of times every second.

If this is true, it is easier to see the continuity between these two realms of awareness. When our awareness enters into form we experience the world in its physical manifestation. When our awareness moves beyond form, we experience pure consciousness as creator of worlds. We are the One Self simultaneously experiencing itself as spirit as well as matter.

When we watch a movie playing in the theater, we forget that it is not a continuous stream of action, but rather a series of images moving across the screen too quickly for the mind to comprehend. Likewise, in the illusion of maya, we forget that we are continually oscillating back and forth between these two states of being.

The function of the rational mind has been to slow down our awareness of time in order to create an apparent continuity of life which we call memory, and which we identify with as *me*. As we learn to experience other levels of the mind, we discover that this sense of *me* is very fluid, and not limited to a single human physical incarnation.

Like the moon, which has no radiance of its own but can easily light up a landscape at night, our human personalities are capable of experiencing and reflecting the light of the Self. How clearly we are capable of reflecting this light has to do with the degree of fixation that we carry within the matrix of our subconscious mind. Ultimately, our task as human beings incarnated on this planet is to move between and simultaneously manifest both these levels of identity.

Walking between the worlds from a shamanic perspective is equivalent to discovering that we can merge the personal and cosmic aspects of our being. *Advaita*, much like *Ilahinoor* and the *Inka* work, offers tools for experiencing this by refining and unifying different aspects of the mind.

CHAPTER 4
THE SUPRAMENTAL FIELD

We usually assume there is a single level of the mind, what we might call the rational mind, and that the sense of reality generated by this level of the mind is the only reality there is.

What if there were other levels of the mind accessible as we learn to bridge between the worlds, each able to perceive and engage with completely different levels of reality?

Our ordinary reality, the middle world, is perceived through the rational level of the mind. We utilize five sense instruments to gather information from this world, and respond to this world. However, since this world is experienced as outside of ourselves, there is a limit of how much information we can receive as well as how much we can influence this reality.

The lower worlds can be accessed through a subliminal field known as the cellular mind. This level of the mind is linked with autonomic functions of the body and subconscious levels of the mind. When the cellular mind operates unconsciously we are beset by traumas, addictions, moods and illnesses capable of creating great distress and suffering. However, when the cellular mind is yoked with higher levels of the mind, we are able to attract and manifest structures of great beauty and power in the outer world.

The upper worlds are accessed through levels of the mind beyond the rational mind, generally referred to as the superconscious realms. An understanding of these realms can be useful in terms of harnessing our full potential, and consciously engineering the next stage of human evolution.

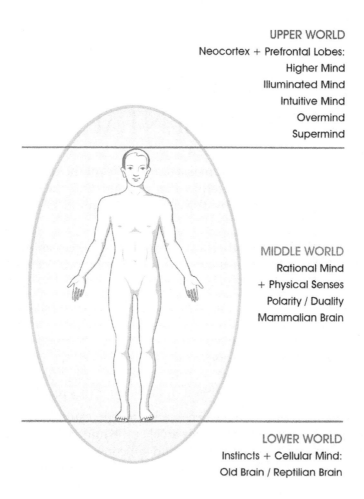

UPPER WORLD
Neocortex + Prefrontal Lobes:
Higher Mind
Illuminated Mind
Intuitive Mind
Overmind
Supermind

MIDDLE WORLD
Rational Mind
+ Physical Senses
Polarity / Duality
Mammalian Brain

LOWER WORLD
Instincts + Cellular Mind:
Old Brain / Reptilian Brain

In *Gaia Luminous,* I refer to the work of the great Indian yogi and mystic, Sri Aurobindo, in mapping these levels of the mind and delineating a path to access them. There are five levels of the mind within the superconscious realms, which I briefly summarize below. There is also the rational mind that most of us are very familiar with, and the cellular mind, which represents the deep elemental wisdom inherent in the superconscious.

The higher mind is witness consciousness. By deliberately quieting the rational mind we learn to choose our path in life. We learn to see from a bird's eye perspective. We are still using logic and reason but the vistas are wider. We are not fixated in emotional dramas or reactivity, and hence can create enough space in the mind to walk the path with heart.

Beyond this is the illumined mind. The doorways between worlds open wider, and our senses become more sensitive. The world becomes more colorful, we learn to listen to the voice of the wind, and there is magic shimmering in all the things we touch.

Next we enter the realm of the intuitive mind. This is not just about intuition in the way we normally use that term. We actually become what we perceive. As the doorways between worlds continue to widen, our sense of separateness dissolves. We learn to feel a person from inside themselves, we learn to shapeshift between forms and realities. Our personal identity is no longer fixed but becomes increasingly permeable.

Beyond this is the overmind. Here we enter the archetypal world of gods and goddesses. The last vestiges of personal ego have emptied out, and we are now identified with cosmic forces which take on a life of their own, creatively channeling through us in powerful ways to serve a divine purpose. This is the realm of cosmic consciousness, generally referred to as enlightenment.

And finally, even beyond the overmind is the Supermind. Sri Aurobindo refers to this level of the mind as supramental consciousness. It is a force of divinity that is entering deep into the collective fields of matter, with the potential of initiating an entirely new wave of creation. This is a level of the mind where the boundaries between the worlds have utterly vanished, where vast evolutionary forces are unleashed within the heart of matter.

Achieving this level of the mind is exceedingly rare, but if we can manage to get there we become capable of collapsing and recreating entire worlds of reality. Entire forces of creation channel through the surrendered ego to serve a planetary or cosmic vision. It is the consciousness of an *avatar*, or a *sixth level human* in the Inka tradition.

Although the supramental field is rarely experienced by humans at this stage of our evolution, there is a collective supramental descent taking place right now. This descent of light has the power to transform our existing matrix of duality into a beautifully refined matrix of unified light. It can transmute the collective *hucha* of a world dangerously out of balance, and use the imminent reversal of planetary magnetic fields to establish a new world age.

From the mind of light can ultimately be built the body of light, a new biology that is able to maintain the infinite power of divinity in multi-dimensional, holographic awareness of all things. Once we achieve the body of light we are no longer subject to the laws of entropy, aging, disease or death. Perhaps, in generations to come, we will be ready for this too.

CHAPTER 5
THE NEUROSCIENCE OF
ENLIGHTENMENT

I f the mind can be regarded as the software of Consciousness, the brain is the hardware.

No matter how good the software is, if our brain and nervous system is not able to process the quality of *sami* flowing through, we will not be able to experience higher states of mind while remaining in the physical body.

Once we understand how the brain works, we can learn to enhance its functions.

Researchers talk about four different functional aspects of the brain, which when linked together, constitutes our nervous system. So let's start with that.

First, there is the reptilian brain. Situated just above the brain stem, this part of the brain is anatomically very similar to that of reptiles and amphibians. It is completely instinctual, and programmed for survival. This part of the brain regulates the autonomic functions of the body, such as breathing, heart rate and body temperature. The flight and fight response is located here.

Next is the mammalian brain, also known as the limbic system. This is the emotional center of the brain, located just below the cerebrum, and consists of the amygdala, hypothalamus and hippocampus. The amygdala is the fear center of the brain, governs our flight and fight response, and is linked with subconscious trauma and memories. It represents Freud's *id*, a primitive consciousness dominated by fear, sex and aggression.

The hippocampus has direct access to memories, as well as to our subconscious history. This could be the part of the brain that actually creates memories. It also uses information from our higher brain centers to determine emotional responses. It is susceptible to free radical and chemical damage caused by trauma and stress, which tends to freeze our ability to respond, and locks us into highly reactive patterns of life.

The hypothalamus is responsible for the regulation of certain metabolic processes and other activities of the autonomic nervous system. One of its important functions is to link the nervous system with the endocrine system through the pituitary gland.

Next comes the neocortex, also known as the new brain. Composed of the two hemispheres, it provides the capacity to develop reason and logic, create art, compose poetry, and plan for the future. If the limbic system represents the *id*, the neocortex represents the *superego*, our ability to balance and override instinctive and emotional impulses with reason and choice.

The prefrontal lobe, located in the front of the brain, is the most recent development in the evolution of our nervous system. It is where individuality and our sense of self developed. It is where we can dream and be creative, search for greater meaning in our lives, and seek for enlightenment.

Our human journey is about learning to synthesize all these functions of the brain. It is about dreaming infinite possibilities while also planting our feet on the earth, feeling the full spectrum of our emotions while also using the mind to plan our path of destiny, being financially responsible while also seeking to grow spiritually, honoring our instincts for survival, sex and security while also choosing to thrive in community based on freedom, altruism and sharing of resources, utilizing the lessons of the past while also dreaming a new world awake.

When Castaneda speaks about following the path with a heart, it includes for me the ability to synthesize our brain functions, and liberate the full potential of our humanness.

The Ilahinoor and Inka work provides tools for building bridges between these various brain functions, and we will explore several of these practices in the following section. But our path to spiritual and emotional maturity is also influenced by our physical state of health, and we cannot ignore this. As we discuss later, this includes our ability to provide the brain with nutrients needed in order to function efficiently, as well as to detoxify the brain from accumulated toxins, chemicals and free radicals.

Our brain is still evolving. As we learn to access higher levels of the mind, this changes our biology, and we evolve corresponding structures within the brain in order to integrate these levels of the mind. Our brain ultimately functions as a receiving station for evolutionary impulses from vast dimensions of consciousness. As we learn to integrate these impulses, it reflects not only in our physical bodies but in the subtle bodies as well.

Our ability to access the upper worlds and lower worlds has to do with building links between the physical body and subtler bodies of light. As these layers of the aura integrate with the physical body, it generates a field of light, or biophotons, within our cells. The stronger this field of biophotons, the healthier and more luminous we become, and the easier we are able to walk between the worlds.

The word *Inka* literally means *luminous*. The Inka *paqos* speak of the *luminous* ones who are coming back now, the true children of the Earth. This is the next species being birthed, *homo luminous*, and it is our privilege to stand between the worlds at this time, witnessing this time of change.

Sri Aurobindo, in his epic poem, Savitri, speaks of the arrival of this new species:

Homo Luminous

I saw them cross the twilight of an age,
The sun-eyed children of a marvelous dawn,
Great creators with wide brows of calm,
The massive barrier-breakers of the world,
Laborers in the quarries of the gods…
The architects of immortality.
Into the fallen human sphere they came
Faces that wore the Immortal's glory still…
Bodies made beautiful by the spirit's light…
Carrying the Dionysian cup of joy
Lips chanting an unknown anthem of the soul
Feet echoing in the corridors of Time
High priests of wisdom, sweetness, might, and bliss
Discoverers of beauty's sunlit ways…
Their tread one day shall change the suffering earth
And justify the light on Nature's face.

(Savitri, pp. 343-4)

PART II

THE JOURNEY

Homo Luminous

Brother Sun, I asked one day

Don't you ever tire

Of spinning endless circles around the sky?

Rising, then setting

Eternal mystery of day and night?

He looked at me then

Gazing soft into my heart

Filling me deep with his light

It is not I that spins through the skies

Creating days and nights he said

Here there is only undying light

Of eternal radiance

All else is perception

See me and you shall see yourself

All shadows are lifted

In noonday light

Once you have seen

No longer can you be a speck

Circling around me

Blowing in the wind

Separate and alone

Be the Sun, be undying light

Yes be a Sun unto yourself

And we shall circle

Always eternally within each other

Kiara Windrider

This next section of the book blends teachings with a series of exercises from the Inka, Ilahinoor, Advaita, and Yogic traditions. Although simple to practice, you will feel yourself connecting with infinite fields of light as you open doorways between the worlds, and as your sense of personal identity expands out beyond the confines of ordinary reality.

My intention is to present these teachings in a way that can be easily learned and practiced.

CHAPTER 6
OCEAN IN THE DROP

S ri Aurobindo's reference to the sun-eyed children of the marvelous dawn touches me deeply. He is referring to divine spirit entering into human form, acting through these bodies, and creating a new species of life within the realm of matter.

Matter is alive, everything is alive, everything always has been alive, except that because of our conditioning and our collective entrapment in the matrix of the middle world, somehow we have lost that connection.

The Q'ero refer to everything as part of a divine flow. There is nothing that is outside this flow, nothing that's not alive. We tend to create a distinction between what's animate and what's inanimate. But all these distinctions are part of the duality we create through the rational mind.

Beyond the middle world, however, there are countless other realms and dimensions. And as we become familiar with these realms and dimensions we recognize that we have never not been *One*. It is just the idea of separateness that's kept us trapped in the illusion of duality.

To release this illusion doesn't take long. We used to think that we had to sit in a cave somewhere meditating for lifetimes. But it's not about more effort.

There is a story about a seeker who goes looking for the perfect master. He finally discovers him sitting in a cave up on the mountain and asks to be apprenticed to him. The master agrees. The student wants to become enlightened, and asks the master how long this would take. "Oh, for you maybe twenty years." The student is agitated. "No, that's too long", he says. "What if I work twice as hard, what if I meditate twice as long?" "In that case," replies the master, "maybe forty years!"

Our journey into light includes our ability to embrace the shadow. As more and more light comes it will naturally bring up more of the shadow, more hucha. We're all dealing with it in these times. Many of us are experiencing this now in a very intense way.

The shadow is the aspect of ourselves that we do not like, that is painful, that keeps us trapped in a certain state of contraction. Most of us come in with some degree of shadow. It's just what this dimension is like so far. It's a collective illusion, it's like in the movie, the matrix. It's a constructed reality that appears to be real.

And the truth is, and even quantum physics is saying this now, that nothing exists out there independent of what's in here. So when I look at you, you don't exist. You are what you are in me, which is how I experience you. And that's my relationship with everything. Because ultimately the idea of separation of the self is an illusion from this perspective.

It's not an illusion from the level of physical consciousness it's a beautiful thing. It's beautiful to have a mind, a body, an ego, a personality that can interact and relate to those around us, to life, to creation. It's a beautiful world. But ultimately there is only one reality, and that's the Self, the One Self with many names.

So when we talk about enlightenment, this is something that need not take long to access. It's a matter of holding that space, entering more deeply into that, and then gradually allowing this space to enter more deeply into the body.

Some of you may be familiar with the beautiful poet Rumi. In Turkey, where I lilved for some years, he is known as *Mevlana,* or beloved teacher. He talks about three stages of disolving. The first stage is where you experience yourself as a drop, and the ocean is out there. And then in the second stage the drop enters into the ocean and experiences itself as the ocean.

And then in the third stage, and this is even more important, the ocean enters into the drop. That's the awakening of the full divine creator energy in the body, in matter, in the interaction with life all around us. We have now become creators. It's no longer the drop separate from the ocean. It's the ocean entering into the drop, entering into the body, so that there's no more separation on that level.

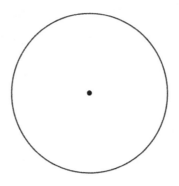

PRACTICE – THE DROP AND THE OCEAN

1. Imagine that the universe is a great big circle. You are a tiny point in the middle of this circle. This is the perspective of the drop.

2. Now imagine that the entire universe is a tiny point, and that you are this great big circle stretching out into infinity. This is the perspective of the ocean.

3. Who are you? Imagine these two identities merging, the great ocean of consciousness pouring into the drop of consciousness expressed as the human self.

4. Notice how you begin to dis-identify from the stories and dramas of life as you recognize yourself as the Self.

CHAPTER 7
THE UPPER WORLD

As mentioned earlier, the Inka work is about learning to build bridges between the upper world, middle world and lower world. Once we do so, we find that can simultaneously experience ourselves as the drop as well as the ocean. The deeply ingrained sense of duality, which generates *hucha* and leads to suffering on so many levels, begins to dissolve.

The three worlds are associated with different levels of the mind. Our access to the lower world is through the cellular mind. It represents the consciousness of the body, and our instinctive relationship with the Earth. The upper world of spirit is accessed through higher levels of the mind, while the middle world, our experience of ordinary reality, is accessed through the rational mind.

As we learn to create bridges between the three worlds, these three levels of the mind can start functioning together, leading to shifts in our perception of reality as well as our ability to influence the world around us.

The basic practice in the Inka tradition is about working with the poqpo, a bubble of energy that surrounds the physical body, what Castaneda referred to as the luminous egg. It is flexible and transparent, and represents the boundary of the middle world. It can also serve as a bridge to non-ordinary states of consciousness.

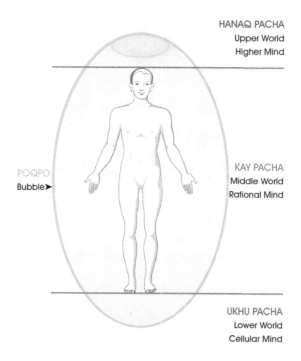

HANAQ PACHA
Upper World
Higher Mind

POQPO
Bubble➤

KAY PACHA
Middle World
Rational Mind

UKHU PACHA
Lower World
Cellular Mind

The bubble normally extends about one or two meters out from the body in all directions. It represents our boundaries, our sense of personal space. It also represents the personal ego, the sense of separate individualized existence that we tend to identify with.

Once we get a sense of our energetic boundaries we can learn to expand our perceptions. We open to the flow of life, and develop a relationship with earth and sky. We experience the universe as a field of living energy, or *sami*, that is constantly moving back and forth through all creation. We understand that we are not separate from this flow, and can therefore learn to direct this flow in order to create harmony and balance. We begin to walk the path with heart by understanding the laws of *ayni*, or reciprocity.

This bubble is not the same as the aura. The aura represents the totality of inter-connected fields, which includes all our subtle bodies, extending all the way out to the causal body or the soul. When fully awakened, this spans the entire cosmos. Initially, however, bring your awareness to a bubble extending about one meter out from the physical body, representing the boundaries of the middle world. This is the world of the rational mind and the physical senses, your sense of who you are as a drop within the ocean.

You then become aware of a window at the very top of this bubble, which represents a gateway into the upper world, the *hanaq pacha*. Like the aperture of a camera, this window can be opened and closed according to need. As you begin to explore the upper world, you learn to open this window with conscious intent, allowing universal *sami* to flow down through the body in response.

There is also a gateway into the lower world, the *ukhu pacha*, which opens through the soles of our feet. Unlike the window above the head, say the Inka, this gate is always open.

The Inka practices are not so much about effort and visualization as about conscious intent. Effort and visualization are functions of the rational mind, but intent engages the cellular mind and the higher mind. The *sami* has its own intelligence which engages these corresponding levels of the mind as it creates a bridge between the worlds.

The nature of *sami* is to flow. Whenever this flow is blocked or stifled, it is referred to as *hucha*. So what they say is that *sami* is constantly flowing through all of life. This is the web of life. We cannot be separate even if we try. But if we try hard enough we think we are separate, and then that creates suffering.

The Inkas say that humans are the only species on this planet, as far as we know, that is capable of generating *hucha*. The way we do this is through fear, which creates resistance or attachments. If we cannot trust the flow of life, if we are holding on to something, whether it's possessions, money, or even belief systems, this stops the flow so that our energy gets stifled. This also then breaks the connection between the upper world and the lower world.

When we are in touch with the upper world there is a constant fluidity. Life moves in surprising ways, synchronistically and powerfully and bountifully. When we stop this flow we become fixated on what we think we know, or think we have, or think is good for us, and then enter into the pseudo world of our own illusion.

So let's move on to a basic practice, known as *samin chakuy*, the downward flow.

PRACTICE – SAMIN CHAKUY

1. Get your feet flat on the ground, taking your shoes off if you want. I find that being barefoot does make a difference, provides a stronger earthing.

2. Take a few deep, relaxing breaths.

3. Imagine around your body now a bubble of light, extending out an arms length in every direction... all the way around you... below you... above you. It's a transparent, flexible, egg shaped bubble, like a soap bubble except permeable and strong.

4. Notice at the very top of this bubble an opening, a window to the sky. This is your doorway to the upper world. You open this window now as wide as you can.

5. You immediately experience a stream of light pouring down from the upper world. It's like being under a waterfall in the jungle, a high frequency of light continuously pouring down through your body, down through your bubble, down through your feet, and into the earth. It's a powerful, electrical stream of light, vibrating at such a high frequency that it begins to stir and release layers of hucha being held in your body, or within the subconscious aspects of your mind.

6. This hucha begins to move down, along with the sami coming down from above. It goes down through your feet and is welcomed by Mother Earth. Don't worry about polluting her. For Mother Earth, hucha is simply compost. She knows how to transmute it, and she welcomes it unconditionally.

7. Stay in this flow for a while, continuing to experience this downward, electrical stream of light. If you're not feeling this

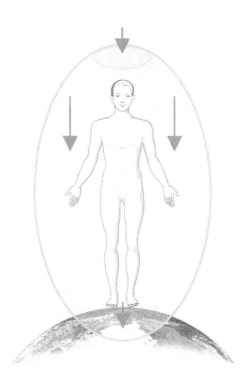

stream as strongly as you would like, just open that window a little bit wider.

8. Notice there is no effort involved. Once the bubble is open it just happens by itself. You are not trying to do anything, not even trying to visualize anything. You simply open the window, connect with the flow of sami, and allow the cellular mind to do what it already knows how to do.

CHAPTER 8
THE LOWER WORLD

A s important as the connection with the upper world is our connection with the lower world. Many on a spiritual path tend to feel more connected with the world of spirit than with the earth. But the earth represents the grounding aspect, which is about being present in your body, and living in trust. You are where you need to be each moment, and are given what you need in that moment. Where there is trust there is fearlessness. You are not ruled by the fear of what people could do to you, what life could do to you. When fully grounded, there is no room for seeing yourself as a victim.

Being grounded is about connecting with the lower world, connecting with cellular intelligence. The body knows things that the rational mind doesn't. As you listen to the body you build a relationship with Pachamama, or Mother Earth, and learn to experience the magic of each ordinary moment. This is the path with heart.

In the samin chakuy practice you are opening a window to the sky. This is an invitation for sami to start flowing through the body and *poqpo* down to the earth. The *sami* that flows down is electrical in nature, a very high frequency. It is blissful in nature and begins to release layers of hucha held in the body as it flows down into the earth.

This initiates the principle of *ayni*. When there is a flow of energy coming down, there is simultaneously a flow of energy going up. Mother earth reciprocates by sending her energy up, through the feet, and up through the body. In contrast to downward electrical energy, this upward flow is magnetic. Magnetic energy is warm and nurturing, life giving and nourishing. It is unconditionally loving and healing. It is associated with the Mother, while the electric energy is associated with the Father.

So as soon as you open the window there is a stream of light that starts pouring down, in response to which there is a return flow of light pouring up. These dual flows, electric and magnetic, move through every single cell of the body. And as these interact within the cells, it creates a subtle matrix of light, which can be experienced as a sense of deep stillness and presence. You're not trying to do anything; all this takes place by itself with the awakening of the cellular mind.

This sense of presence starts moving through the body, through the bubble, then out beyond the bubble, until you eventually feel like you become one with the earth, and out through the cosmos. Ultimately you experience yourself extending beyond the boundaries of time and space to the ground of Being where you are simply undivided Consciousness. You become the great cosmic Ocean. But there is no duality here. You experience yourself as the Universe, while at the same time remaining grounded in the body, more fully present than ever.

PRACTICE – SAYWA CHAKUY

1. Begin with an awareness of the bubble, extending an arms length out all around you.

2. Become aware of the window on top of this bubble, and open this window as wide as you can. You immediately begin to experience the universal electrical sami flowing down like a mighty stream of light. It flows through the entire wasi (poqpo plus physical body), releasing to the earth whatever hucha is ready to be released.

3. And now, in response to the downward flow, become aware of an answering stream, a wave of light that comes up from mother earth, directly up through the soles of the feet, and then moves

up through every cell of the body, up through the bubble, up through the window, and up to the sky.

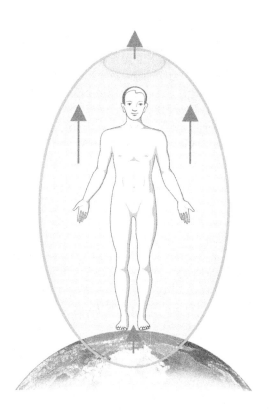

4. This sami from the earth is magnetic in nature. It feels warm, healing, nourishing, loving, deeply grounding. There is a sense of being totally supported and welcome on this earth. Experience this flow as a warm geyser coming up from the earth, moving up through the soles of your feet, and all the way up through the body.

Again, this happens by itself. You're learning to connect with the cellular mind, which already knows all these things.

5. Notice how this stream feels for you. You become aware now that both these streams are moving simultaneously on their own, streaming through every cell of the body. And as they interact within the cells of the body, you begin to experience a stillness, a presence, a sense of expansion. As this matrix of light gets established, you feel yourself stretching further and further out through time and space, out through the planet, through the solar system, through multiple galaxies, out to the very boundaries of time and space, and then beyond. You begin to experience yourself as the Self, permeating the entire Cosmos while at the same time deeply present and anchored within the physical body.

6. And now, while keeping that window open, slowly open your eyes. Become aware that you are still in that expanded flow of light. As long as the window is open, you are still connected with the electric and magnetic streams. You don't have to be in a meditative state to be connected with the upper and lower worlds. Its just a natural part of being you could be talking walking driving sleeping, and still be in the flow between worlds.

7. At first you may find that the window automatically closes after a while because the body needs to integrate this new energy. But after a while you can keep this window open. As long as the two flows are balanced, there are no limits to how far outwards you can expand, and how deeply inwards you can discover your own divine presence.

CHAPTER 9
WALKING BETWEEN THE WORLDS

I**s it possible to keep the window open through all the activities of life? Is it possible to walk with an awareness of all the worlds at all times?

When people first begin to do this practice they often feel 'stoned'. There is a feeling of bliss, accompanied with subtle vibrations, strong heat, pressure, and a deep stillness in the body, which makes it difficult to think or move. There is a sense of being at one with all things, a profound peace knowing you can trust mother Earth and the universe, and comfort in surrendering to the deep guiding force behind all experiences of life. As deep core layers of *hucha* are released, people experience various sorts of emotional release. Kundalini begins to awaken, opening up access to higher levels of the mind.

As you access different levels of the mind, the doors of perception open. You begin to view the world from a *big picture* perspective. You start to open up clairvoyant, clairsentient, and clairaudient senses. And you begin to experience how everything you perceive becomes a part of you.

When I look at you, I become you and you become me. I see the same light in you that I experience in myself. When I look at a tree or a landscape, I become part of it, and it becomes part of me. There is no separation in this flow of consciousness. And where there is no separation, there is no guilt, no shame, no judgment, no fear, only a sense of curiosity and discovery in all things.

The Q'ero people did not have plastic toys and video games. Children were taught early on to open the bubble and experience all of nature directly, whether plants, animals, mountains, birds or the living presence of the earth. People sometimes refer to this as *channeling,* but this is a natural ability we can all learn to practice. We are not accessing anything outside of ourselves; we are simply expanding our bubble to include larger fields of life. Shamans sometimes refer to this ability as *shape shifting*.

You cannot shape shift from a place of personal ego. But as you connect the *kai pacha* with the *hanaq pacha* and the *ukhu pacha,* you experience yourself not so much as a fixed entity but as a stream of consciousness. From this place, it can become simple and fun.

We assume that reality is the same for all people. But our idea of reality is more a consensus we share than something that has reality on its own. Our consensus reality is shaped by our culture, our television shows, our belief systems. Meanwhile, the consensus reality of the Inka people, the aboriginal people, is completely different. Their worldview is different, their belief system is different, so their reality is different because reality is a projection of our internal worldviews and conditioning.

Some of you may know the story of when Columbus and his crew came to the new world. The native people couldn't see ships that big because it wasn't in their worldview. And the first to see them was the shaman who was used to expanding his worldview. And once he could see then the others could see them too!

What are we not seeing right now? Maybe a cat would experience this same reality very differently, as would a butterfly, an earthworm or a salamander. There could be all kinds of creatures around us that we cannot see yet because they don't exist within our worldview. So shape shifting means being sensitive to different worldviews, different perspectives, and to honor and appreciate them all.

As with other Inka practices, you begin by opening the window, experiencing the electrical and magnetic streams moving and interacting through the entire sawi. Once you begin to feel the loosening of your personal identity, invite your helpers, guides or anyone you wish to communicate with into the bubble. Notice the shifts in sense perception. What do you see, feel, hear, smell, taste? Notice your sense of weight, shape and size. Imagine yourself experiencing the world from this new perspective. Is there a message or a healing gift that you receive? What can you offer back? How does this encounter transform your relationship with the world?

PRACTICE – SHAPE SHIFTING

1. Imagine yourself inside your bubble of light. Open this bubble now and begin to experience an electrical stream of light pouring down through the wasi and into the earth. As this stream of sami gets stronger it releases any hucha that needs to be released, carrying it down to be transmuted by mother earth.

2. Become aware now of a magnetic stream of light that moves up from the earth in response. You feel this in the bottoms of your feet, and then it continues to move up all the way through your wasi, up through the window and back to the sky.

3. As you experience both these streams simultaneously now, you allow them to simply continue flowing on their own, linking you with sky and earth, hanaq pacha and ukhu pacha.

4. And now imagine a condor flying up in the sky. He is a guardian of the upper world. Invite that condor in through the window and into your bubble. What happens in your energy bodies? What happens with your sense of vision? What's your relationship with the sky? How do you feel kinesthetically? Is there a message? Become the condor completely… Now thank the condor, say goodbye to him, and watch him fly off into the sky. Feel again your human identity.

5. And now imagine you are walking through the jungle and encounter a jaguar. She is a guardian for the middle world. Invite the jaguar in through the window and into your bubble. Notice what happens. How do you experience your sense of hearing, or smell? How do you feel your connection with the earth, and with

the planetary web of life? What's your sense of who you are? What emotions come up for you? Become the jaguar completely... Now thank the jaguar, say goodbye to her, and watch her wander back into the jungle. Feel again your human identity.

6. And now imagine in front of you a rattlesnake, coiled under a rock. Perhaps you experience some trepidation at first, and then you simply invite him into your bubble as a brother, as a sister. You become the rattlesnake. Notice your sense of touch, your response to the vibrations of the earth. What do you feel in your spine? What happens to the kundalini within your energy body? What's your connection with earth and sky? Now thank the rattlesnake, say goodbye to her. Feel again your human identity.

7. And now imagine climbing your favorite mountain. Invite this mountain into your bubble, and notice how that feels, the sense of form, the sense of weight, the sense of being, the sense of time. Thank this mountain, say goodbye to him, return to your human identity.

8. And now imagine you are under a night sky, brilliant with stars. You see the entire Milky Way up above you. And you fix upon one single star up in the sky, one star that draws you. And invite that star into your bubble, this beautiful brilliant creation in the form of a star. Notice how you experience that in your field, in your energy bodies, your kundalini channels. You become that star. Notice how you shine. What is your sense of space... and time? Thank the star now, say goodbye... and reconnect with your human identity.

9. Notice that your human identity is more fluid now, not quite so fixed anymore. You experience yourself as consciousness moving through human form, but not identified exclusively as a human.

CHAPTER 10
PACHAMAMA

While many spiritual traditions emphasize our connection with the upper worlds, shamanic cultures worldwide tend to emphasize our relationship with the lower worlds. Why so much emphasis on this connection with the Earth?

The Inkas, like other indigenous people, see the earth as a living system, which the English biologist James Lovelock, refers to as *Gaia*. As human beings we have the privilege to participate in this beautifully connected web of life, not as dominators but as guardians. The moment we see ourselves on top of some hypothetical ladder of evolution with some imagined right to own and conquer the wildness of nature, we have already separated ourselves from Her. The sad and painful consequences of this separation are not difficult to observe.

Let me define Gaia. We think of Gaia as the earth. But She is much more than that. Gaia is the highly conscious, intelligent being who has given rise to all species on this planet. We would not be here without her invitation. The Q'ero people refer to her as *Pachamama*.

Mother earth is *Pachamama*. But *Pachamama* literally means Cosmic Mother. Our bodies are also *Pachamama*. Each of us is *Pachamama*. The sun, the stars, the galaxy are also *Pachamama*. It's not Gaia as one polarity with Cosmos as the other polarity. All of it is the Cosmic Mother through which we find ourselves expressed in Creation.

As long as I see myself as separate from *Pachamama*, the rational mind is in charge. But evolution demands more. The rational mind is finding its proper place in union with the cellular mind, in union with the higher mind. The rational mind is essential to function in the physical world. It's a beautiful thing. But if we focus exclusively on this we have cut ourselves off from the rest of creation.

There is a word in the Quechua language, *salka*, which means *wildness*. Wildness is the wolf that hunts in the forest, the eagle that soars across the skies, the buffalo that roams the prairies. Wildness is nature in its lush fertile bounty. Wildness is the heart that is untamed, and dares to be free. Wildness is the ability to think outside the box, to dream new possibilities, to follow our bliss. Have we lost our salka in the predictable confinement of our orderly existence, divorced from the magic of creation, removed from the invisible worlds that give us life and meaning?

When did we lose touch with Pachamama and become slaves to an increasingly sterile world? When did we learn to measure a forest in terms of lumber, or a beautiful landscape by its real estate value? When did we learn to measure our own worth in terms of empty roles and meaningless rules? When did we swap our right to happiness for a higher gross national product? Have we traded wildness for safety, freedom for security, and beauty for predictability?

PRACTICE – SEEKING SALKA

1. Take a day off for yourself, perhaps even longer if you can. Find a place in nature that inspires you. Take a journal along.

2. Open the window above, and make a connection with sky and earth. Invite your council of helpers, teachers and guides into your bubble. Become aware of the spirits of nature all around you. Slow down your thoughts and allow these beings to introduce themselves through the pages of your journal. What do they wish to say?

3. Now take some time to contemplate your life's journey, highlighting the moments that have brought you greatest joy, beauty, love and fulfillment. Ask yourself how well you have lived your life. What are you passionate about? How many lives have you touched? What have you learned about love? If you died today, what would people remember you for? Have you dared to pursue your dreams? Have you followed the path with a heart?

4. Ask yourself now where you have compromised your heart, and where you have become domesticated. Recognizing that we all require a balance of domestication to function in human society, what would this balance look like for you? Have you allowed your need for safety and comfort to override your need for mystery and wildness? How would you shape your life differently if you could?

5. The tragedy of our times is that our need to domesticate the world has brought us close to planetary suicide. How can we restore the balance of ayni now, becoming givers rather than takers, guardians rather than exterminators? Recognizing that you are one strand in a planetary web of life, what skills and perspectives could you offer in service to *Pachamama*, the greater whole?

6. The saddest aspect of losing touch with our salka is that we have become numb to the voice of spirit that moves through all things. We have learned to settle for lives of quiet desperation, knowing that something is missing, but not being able to understand why. We have built walls within our psyche to protect ourselves from the impact of soul denying choices, and trapped ourselves in prisons of our own making. How would you start taking these walls down? How do you escape the prison of an overly domesticated mind?

7. Take time with these questions. Let them speak to your heart. Then set your journal aside and lay down with your hands and belly touching the earth. Breathe deeply and rhythmically. Speak directly to Pachamama and listen to her speaking back.

CHAPTER 11
CETACEAN EXPERIENCES

I feel fortunate to have found my own *path with a heart* early in life. As a teenager growing up in the mountains of South India, I found great joy in hiking the wilderness trails with my fellow classmates. One day I fell 60 meters down a waterfall, and managed to survive. That experience moved me to explore the deeper meaning of my life, which came with a commitment to seek wildness and freedom, no matter what.

I did not know the word *salka* then, but I had started to read Castaneda, and knew there was nothing I wanted more than to follow this path with a heart.

Years later, I found myself in Hawaii, where I spent many months swimming and interacting with wild spinner dolphins. It was a magical time, and I found that the longer I spent with them the more my sense of personal identity began to drop away.

What does it mean to incarnate in a human body? We have so many ideas, thoughts and concepts about what this means, much of it based on a seeming continuity of memory, or based on roles we have learned to play out in the world. What happens when these ideas and roles begin to drop away?

Many of us have had peak experiences where our concepts and memories of the past dissolve, and we are simply immersed in the present moment, open and connected with the spontaneous flow of life as it rises and falls away. We forget our human roles, and are no longer identified with a story. We simply enter a field of gratitude, joy, and humility.

This is what I found myself experiencing in the presence of these dolphins. They radiated a field of spontaneous joyful presence, and I found myself entering into this. There were times when I no longer felt identified as human, because the dolphins certainly did not identify with being dolphins. It loosened up the fixed sense of self that I had carried around with myself all these years, and it was a beautiful and liberating experience.

And then one day I had an experience with humpback whales. I entered the ocean as usual, but didn't notice any dolphins that day. Then I noticed a huge spout of water. My heart leaped as I recognized a humpback whale in the distance. I swam out to where I had seen the spout, but by the time i arrived there was only an empty ocean. I closed my eyes and called on them as I had learned to do with dolphins, and as I opened them a few minutes later, was amazed to find a mother whale a few meters directly beneath, with her baby swimming in and around between us.

I felt a moment of panic as I realized the immensity of her size and the proximity of her presence. This quickly dissipated however as I realized how attentive she was to my frail human form. As I surrendered to the moment I experienced a powerful transmission of light and energy and love. This transmission seemed to enter my body through an area in the back of my head, triggering a gradual expansion of my sense of self.

She stayed in place for about 20 minutes, during which I felt like my body dissolved and became the earth. I could no longer sense my physical form separate from the planet, Gaia.

It was an ecstatic experience. I could still feel myself as Kiara, but was at the same time blended with Gaia, as one cell within the body of the earth. The distinction between personal self and planetary self became fuzzy and blurred.

I was incarnate in a human body, but was not identified with being human anymore. I was not the personal self I had spent a lifetime developing. The stories created by my mind, the paths that I had walked, the places I had been, the people whom I had met, all this had nothing to do with who I was. The whales had transported me into a dimension where I felt myself as Gaia first, and only then as the human being who called himself Kiara.

Later, when I was able to think, I realized this is how the whales experience reality. Their physiology is designed to experience oneness. As I attuned to the area behind the back of my head, I felt I was being given a new understanding of the human energy system, that this 'whale chakra' represented a new center of consciousness from anything I had known before.

I have come across many references to a race of humans that existed before our own species whose skulls were elongated towards the back. It is likely that this race had access to capacities beyond our own, and I have wondered if they were the ones who built the ancient pyramids and giant monuments that have been excavated around the world. Was this region behind the back of the head part of the energy system of this race of beings, perhaps far more advanced than our current species in certain ways? And could we learn to activate this same etheric chakra within our own bodies?

PRACTICE – ACTIVATING THE WHALE CHAKRA

1. Turn on whale or dolphin music, while inviting them to join you energetically.

2. Bring your attention to a region behind the back of your head, perhaps extending 20 or 30 centimeters out.

3. With your feet grounded on the earth, and hands reaching up to the sky, breathe into this energetic center until you feel an expansion of consciousness.

4. Continue until you feel yourself expanding out to the boundaries of the earth, and beyond.

CHAPTER 12
THE ILAHINOOR BRIDGE

My experiences with whales and dolphins in Hawaii were spontaneous events, arising from the love I felt for these incredible beings. I had not been seeking to enter into meditative states, or merge with Gaia through any particular practices. I had experienced these states from time to time during my meditation practices or shamanic ceremonies, but never to this extent.

But once I recognized that it was possible to do so, I yearned to make this more a part of my life, and intentionally began to develop a relationship with Mama Gaia, as I began to call her. It wasn't any one practice or tradition, just an awareness of Earth as a living web of life. The Cherokees talk about 'walking softly upon the Earth'. It was an understanding that Her needs were more important than my own, that I was placed on this Earth as a guardian and protector for all life, and that living in service to this was my greatest joy.

I lived in Mt Shasta for some years, and learned to relate to her as an *apu*, a mountain spirit with vast intelligence and power. I spent time swimming in mountain lakes and camping in alpine meadows, learned to develop relationships with the *devas* and elemental kingdoms, occasionally feeling the presence of vast beings of light in those higher vibrational frequencies.

Our belief in separation has too often kept us in survival mode, where all we know is to take from the earth without the ability to give back. What does it mean to live in the circle of life, to celebrate the living earth, to develop relationships with the invisible worlds of spirit?

Just as I had experienced with the whales and dolphins in Hawaii, connecting with these kingdoms of life was not so much about expecting some kind of verbal communication, but joining essence as we expanded together into a single awareness of presence. It was an exhilarating journey.

I'm going to fast forward a few years in time now. I eventually left the United States, where I had spent the past twenty years of my life, and found myself in Turkey. It was a land of incredible beauty and diversity, a bridge between East and West, and I felt immediately at home.

During this time I had also become fascinated by Egyptian mythology, recognizing the various gods and goddesses in that ancient tradition as archetypal energies that existed within each of us. One day, as I was sharing some healing practices with a small group of students on the Aegean coast, I felt the presence of *Ra*, one of the deities related to the Sun.

The energy in the room became immensely strong. Speaking of the energies of the new times, he said we were embarking on a collective journey of awakening. He related this to mysterious energies that were pouring in from the center of the galaxy, and said that if we could anchor these energies in the body we could learn to merge the physical body with higher bodies of light, just as in the ancient mystery traditions, where pyramids were used to focus cosmic energy and ultimately immortalize the physical body.

The difference, he said, is that whereas only a select few were chosen to walk the path of mastery in those early days, these were the times of collective initiation, and that we were invited now to transmute the biology of our entire human species.

My exploration of *integral yoga*, the path of supramental descent taught by Sri Aurobindo, had been pointing me in a very similar direction, so I immediately felt a resonance with what he was communicating. In the course of the next few days, we were taught how to work with specific centers in the brain to create bridges in consciousness.

There are different parts of the brain that are linked with different centers of consciousness. There is the high self, middle self and low self, each of which is linked with a different part of the brain, and also linked with the three worlds in shamanic traditions. Egyptian psychology, like the *Huna* tradition of Hawaii, is about learning to interact between three aspects of our being.

The low self, or the subconscious level of the mind, is associated with the limbic center, deep inside the brain stem. The high self, or superconscious mind, is related to chakras, nadis and meridians within the subtle bodies. The middle self is associated with the neocortex and the rational mind. We were taught how to unify these three levels of the mind through a very simple practice.

Ilahinoor, as mentioned earlier, refers to a field of *divine light* that has the specific function of preparing us for evolutionary change. It is linked somehow with cosmic rays and gamma rays pouring in from the center of the galaxy during these times, and also perhaps to the descent of supramental light that Sri Aurobindo refers to. Our intention is to channel this highly refined field of light through our bodies and into the Earth, where it can also serve Gaia in her own evolutionary journey.

PRACTICE – ILAHINOOR BRIDGE

Choose a partner. You will take turns giving and receiving. This practice can also be modified for doing a self-treatment.

1. Invoke the Ilahinoor field in whatever way you wish, recognizing that it is a highly refined field of light with its own intelligence and evolutionary purpose.

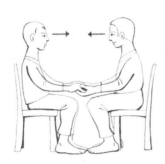

2. Take a couple of minutes to establish eye contact. The eyes are the windows of the soul, and gazing provides a means for quickly creating a soul merge.

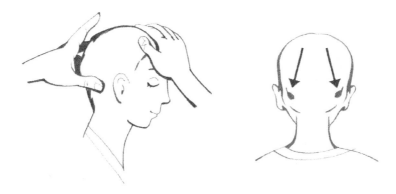

3. Standing to either side of your partner, place one hand on the back of your partner's head, with two fingers holding the Ilahinoor points located about 2 or 3 cm above the occipital ridge. This is an access point into the limbic system, and often somewhat sensitive to touch.

4. The palm of the other hand is placed over the forehead of your partner, with fingers extending up over the crown. This connection between the limbic system and the prefrontal lobes is known as the Ilahinoor bridge.

5. Allow the energy to move between these two centers, linking subconscious and superconscious aspects of their being. Wait until you experience a pulse between them, indicating that the connection has been made.

6. Once you feel the pulse, move the hand on forehead down to the front of the heart chakra, again waiting until you experience a pulse.

7. The other hand then moves to the back of the heart, while you once again wait for the pulse.

8. Continue down to the front of the belly with one hand, while the other remains behind the heart. Wait for the pulse.

9. The other hand moves to the small of the back, while you once again wait for the pulse.

10. Give your partner as much time as needed to integrate, recognizing that this has been a deep initiation. There could be a variety of responses from the body, including heat, trembling and emotional releases. There is often a sense of deep peace, silence, and ecstasy.

Note: The Ilahinoor bridge can also be performed on your own, and is very soothing for the nervous system. You may continue on to create a connection with the heart and then the belly if you wish. If you have difficulty placing a hand on the back of your own heart, simply place both hands over the front. The same goes for the belly.

The Ilahinoor bridge will be followed up in the next few chapters with teachings on the merkaba and the tube of light. A complete Ilahinoor treatment will be demonstrated in Chapter 15.

CHAPTER 13
THE INNER CHILD

I shared earlier the experience I had with the whales in Hawaii, where I became aware of a chakra in the back of the head. Once this was awakened, I found myself expanding past the human self to experience my identity with Pachamama, Gaia, the Cosmic Self.

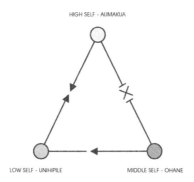

The Ilahinoor initiations in Turkey helped me understand how we could all access the Cosmic Self in a structured way. Perhaps a more detailed explanation of the Hawaiian Huna teachings could be useful in integrating this expanded aspect of being.

The high self in this tradition is known as *aumakua*. The middle self is the *ohane*. The low self is the *unihipile*. The *ohane* represents the conscious personality, while the *aumakua* and *unihipile* represent the superconscious and subconscious aspects of our being.

These could also be interpreted as the human, angelic and elemental aspects of our being. The Kahunas teach that the *ohane* cannot communicate directly with the *aumakua*. We may develop an intellectual understanding of God or the Universe, however we define this, but it is not a direct experience unless we first learn to communicate with the *unihipile*.

The *unihipile* is in constant communication with the *aumakua*. As we learn from the Inka work, the upper world and the lower world are connected through the laws of *ayni*, and you cannot access one without also accessing the other. The cellular mind and the higher mind are always in touch.

In other words, the only way for the rational mind to access the higher mind is through the cellular mind. Or using the language of psychology, the only way the human self can access the divine presence is through the inner child.

The inner child is an aspect of the subconscious mind. When we talk about healing the inner child we are talking about accepting the disowned aspects of ourselves. Our social conditioning, drilled into our subconscious mind from the time we enter incarnation, reminds us over and over again that we are not good enough, not beautiful enough, not smart enough, not loving enough.

Our religious conditioning, also drilled into our subconscious mind from early childhood, tells us that there is something wrong with us, that we are somehow flawed, separated, or sinful. We are taught to adhere to strict rules of morality rather than trusting our own natural instincts for love.

All this forces us to play certain roles in order to justify our existence. The *salka* of our natural self gradually becomes domesticated as we learn to become upright and honorable members of society. Our belief systems adjust to ingrained social conditioning as we create all kinds of judgments and hierarchies within our minds about right and wrong, good and bad, desirable and undesirable.

We become trapped in a loop where our social conditioning creates limiting belief systems, which diminish our perceptions of reality, which leads to a sense of isolation and separation, which gets inherited down through our cultural matrix to the next generation. Over the course of generations this becomes locked into our DNA.

Our conditioning and beliefs are essentially layers of imprinting that get woven into the subconscious matrix of the *unihipile* as *hucha,* heavy energy that distorts the field of oneness. It eventually becomes deeply ingrained into the collective energy field as a matrix of duality, which appears to have a reality of its own.

From the perspective of the *aumakua,* there is only a single undivided flow of *sami* that moves through all things. This *sami* is *salka,* inspiring, wild and free. It seeks only the highest good for all creation. The human self is not separate from the infinite divine flow that permeates the entire cosmos. There are no limits, except the limits we impose on ourselves. Healing the inner child from the perspective of the *aumakua* is simply about releasing the *hucha* that keeps it trapped in separation and fear, the conditioning that prevents us from trusting the wildness of divine flow.

The kahunas say that the *unihipile* is already connected with the *aumakua* at all times, and it is only our limiting belief systems which creates the illusion that we are separate. If the illusion of separation is a mental program we can change this program. We can learn to make friends with the *unihipile* and regain our identity as the *aumakua.*

We must be willing to enter the shadow world, going into aspects of ourselves that have been disowned, denied, repressed, fragmented or hurt. We go into this subconscious territory, not in judgment or trepidation, but with the power of the *aumakua,* knowing who we are, and embracing ourselves fully.

It is not so much the *unihipile,* but our relationship with the *unihipile,* that requires healing. In our willingness to embrace everything that we have disowned about ourselves, our light as well as our shadow, we open ourselves to an expanded sense of identity. The three worlds have come together. We are no longer trapped in the conditioned identity of the *ohane*, but are able to experience the *aumakua* as our deeper, magical Self.

When we connect with this deeper magical Self, there is a spontaneity, trust, playfulness and joy that begins to flow through our life. The Inkas refer to this as *pooklay*. Dolphins and whales seem to express this pooklay very naturally, but all animal species experience themselves as a spontaneous flow of *sami,* and we can learn to relate with them and each other in the same way. This is what healing the inner child is about.

PRACTICE – HEALING THE INNER CHILD

1. Open the window above your head, and experience the connection between the worlds, as electrical and magnetic streams of *sami* interact to create a matrix of flowing light. Feel the living power of earth and sky as a child of the universe.

2. Become aware of layers of conditioning in your life. What are the ways you have allowed fragmentation, fear and illusion into your life? Is there something that is specifically showing up in this moment? As you identify layers of *hucha*, notice where you feel this in your body. Remember that *hucha* is not something negative, just *sami* that has forgotten how to flow. Hence there is no need for judgment, only awareness and understanding.

3. Invoke the field of divine light, and take a few minutes to activate the Ilahinoor bridge on yourself, continuing on to link heart and belly.

4. As you connect these centers, feel a unification between *aumakua, ohane* and *unihipile.* Notice the sense of peace, expansion and joy that follows.

CHAPTER 14
THE MERKABA

The three centers of identity, *aumakua, ohane,* and *unihipile,* roughly corresponding with the head, heart and belly belly, and could be perceived as the angelic, human and elemental aspects of our being. They also correspond with the causal, subtle, and physical bodies, referring to our journey of incarnation. In the Egyptian tradition they are known as the *ba,* the *ka* and the *khat.*

There are levels of the mind linked with each of these major divisions. The causal body is linked with superconscious levels of the mind. The subtle body is linked with conscious levels of the mind. The physical body is linked with subconscious levels of the mind. You could likewise connect the three shamanic worlds with these three centers of identity.

In the Hindu tradition, the essential self is known as the *atman.* This is the spirit that moves through all things. When this *atman* wishes to incarnate in the physical world, it creates a succession of bodies to express itself, starting with the causal body, then the subtle body, and finally the physical body.

The causal body is also known as the soul. This is where our sense of individuality begins. The soul, just like spirit, is eternal. The difference is that while spirit is an expression of the formless aspect of the Self, the soul is expressed within the context of creation, within time and space.

Each individualized soul, whether referring to a galaxy, star, planet or human, cycles in and out of physical existence through a series of incarnations. However, this is not a strictly linear process, since from a shamanic perspective all matter is constantly blinking in and out of physical existence trillions of times every second.

As we incarnate, the causal body works with the process of natural evolution to create a physical body. Through the journey of conception and birth, the soul gradually becomes anchored to the physical body, and develops a subtle body based on cumulative impressions, feelings, thoughts, and subconscious tendencies.

Our sense of identity, while appearing to operate within the physical body, is actually held within the subtle body. This is the personal *ego*, a field of thoughts, feelings, memories and perceptions that creates a sense of *me*, an entity existing within time and space and separate from the rest of the world.

When the physical body dies, we discover that we still exist, but our sense of identity has now transferred from a physical body into a subtle body, which has its own range of senses organs and perceptions, linked with worlds and dimensions that are equally real. Eventually, the subtle body is absorbed into the causal body, where we get to experience a rest phase before planning out the next incarnation.

There is a sense of identity, held within the causal body, which transcends any single incarnation. While much more fluid than the personal ego, it still carries a sense of unique existence. We don't need to leave the physical body in order to experience our soul identity. As we learn to bridge the worlds, these two levels of identity merge and function as one. Beyond the soul, there is simply the Self, the undifferentiated Spirit that moves through all things. Everything else is only a reflection of this.

Our journey of awakening is to remember who we are as the Self, and to allow this awareness of the Self to flow easily between the subtle body and the causal body, even to move past the causal body and experience larger realms of identity as planetary consciousness, as galactic consciousness and as cosmic consciousness.

The merkaba is the link between all these levels of identity. It is roughly correlated with what's known as the aura. The bubble, or luminous egg, as initially used in the Inka tradition, represents the boundaries of the personal ego. We find that as we open the doorways between the worlds, this very quickly takes us beyond the personal ego into larger realms of identity.

In the ancient Egyptian mystery schools, the physical body was known as the *khat*. The subtle body was the *ka*, and the causal body was the *ba*. Thus the *merkaba* teachings were about merging the physical body with the subtle and causal bodies.

There are concentric layers of the aura, all centered around the physical body, but extending further and further out into the cosmos. These layers are not separate from each other but are constantly interpenetrating and interacting with each other, as well as with the endless fields of life all around us.

The *merkaba* represents the sum total of our auric field. It is a geometrical field, as are all fields within creation, and include subtle electrical and magnetic forces. It generally takes the form of a *tube torus*, which is the basic geometry shared by all electromagnetic fields, from atoms to stars to galaxies, including each of us incarnated here on this planet.

Some teachers speak of the *merkaba* as a star tetrahedron, moving as a counter rotational field around the vertical axis of the body. This is accurate as far as it goes, but it is also far more. There are specific geometries associated with each of our bodies, and the merkaba includes all of them.

I had a visual experience of this during a three week darkness retreat at an *ayurvedic* center in India, where I participated in a rejuvenation process that goes back to ancient times. In the old days there were yogis who lived and meditated in seclusion up in the high mountains. Once every seventy or eighty years they would come down from their mountain caves and go through a process called *kayakalpa*, which means rejuvenation of the body.

Ingesting certain herbs, including alchemized gold, they would spend anywhere from a month to nine months in total darkness. During this time the endocrine system would get highly stimulated through the third eye, initiating a rejuvenation process. Their teeth would fall out, their nails would fall out, and their hair would fall out... after which an entirely new set of teeth and hair and bones would grow back. They would eventually emerge from this hibernation looking like they were twenty or thirty years old. It's an amazing process, and humans, as well as some other animals, are capable of this.

During my mini kayakalpa, I experienced a profound activation of the third eye, and was able to occasionally see some of the subtle geometries of the *merkaba*. These fields were infinitely complex and beautiful, filaments of light extending in all directions, and constantly changing in response to my thoughts and intentions.

I noticed also that my merkaba was linked with other fields of life around me. One day I had been working with activating the merkaba with a sequence of yogic breaths. That night a mighty vortex of wind came through the village, and the doctor came running in the next day commenting on how unusual this was. I didn't make a connection then, but a few days later I was teaching a friend of mine this merkaba breath, and the same thing happened again.

Similar sorts of phenomena often take place when I teach the merkaba work, especially in areas where energetic clearing is needed. We are all connected, and our merkabas are capable of influencing elemental powers all around us. Our planet has its own merkaba field, and as we connect with this, deep collective transformations begin to happen.

You can do the following practice either with a partner or on your own. As you become adept at activating the merkaba you can learn to connect with larger fields out in nature, and even with the planetary merkaba.

PRACTICE – ACTIVATING THE MERKABA

This practice is described here for working with a partner. You could be sitting across from each other, or even done long

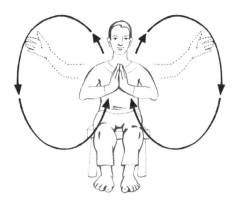

distance. The same practice can be modified for activating your own merkaba.

1. As usual, begin with opening the doorway between the worlds. If your partner is familiar with the Inka work, you can choose to open the windows to the upper world together, and experience the downward and upward flows streaming through each of you.

2. Bring the palms of your hands together over your heart. Invoke the intelligence of the cellular mind, which in many respects is far greater than the rational mind.

3. You are now going to activate the merkaba of your partner, using your intent. While your partner continues to sit receptively with eyes closed, you make an aka (energetic) connection between your own heart and your partner's heart. Wait a minute or two until this connection feels strong.

4. You will use intent, along with breath, to activate the merkaba, which moves out like a *tube torus* from your partner's heart center, and out through their aura. There will be three breaths. With each breath, you take a deep inhale, feel for the right moment, and then forcefully expel your breath while moving your hands in a rapid circular motion, starting from your heart chakra, then moving up, around and back to your heart.

5. With the first breath, your intent is to activate the receiver's merkaba spinning in a counter-clockwise direction. Feel for the right moment, and expel your breath forcefully.

6. With the second breath, your intent is to activate the merkaba spinning in a clockwise direction. Feel for the right moment, and expel your breath forcefully.

7. With the third breath, as these counter-rotational fields start spinning faster and faster, your intent is to activate the merkaba fully, going out as far as it is capable of going at this time. Feel for the right moment, and expel your breath forcefully.

8. Allow time to integrate the experience.

CHAPTER 15
AN ILAHINOOR
SEQUENCE

We are going to put some of the different steps together now to create a basic Ilahinoor sequence. Remember that we are not trying to generate something from the rational mind here, but connecting with a field of light that has its own intelligence and purpose.

The first step in any of these practices is to open the doorway between the worlds. All you require is a basic intent, and the cellular mind then takes over. As the body gets used to the higher frequencies of *sami,* the window can be left open for longer and longer periods, until eventually it becomes possible to keep the window open at all times, hence living in a constant flow of multi-dimensional awareness.

We next move on to create some Ilahinoor connections. If you are working with a partner, decide who goes first. You can also do the sequence on yourself, modifying the sequence as needed.

You begin with invoking the Ilahinoor field, however this works for you. You could also invite any teachers, guides, angels, masters or nature spirits you wish.

Sitting across from each other, you start with a soul merge, gazing into each other's eyes until you establish soul contact. You will feel a distinct shift in the vibrational frequency. Some people may not feel comfortable with direct gazing at first, in which case this step is optional.

You then proceed with the Ilahinoor bridge. The giver comes over to the side of the person receiving, making the connection between the Ilahinoor points in the back of the head and the prefrontal cortex. Proceed to the contacts at the front and back of the heart, then front and back of the belly.

You then activate the whale chakra. Here you are directing energy through the little finger of one hand, through the third eye and then into the whale chakra situated about 20 to 30 centimeters behind the back of the head. The little finger, which includes the heart and small intestine meridians, represents the fire element.

As you point this finger, also known as the *pinkie*, into the third eye region, you are activating the kundalini energies latent within the endocrine system, with the intention for activating the whale chakra. Rather than directly touching the forehead, the finger is held about one or two centimeters away from the body. Experiment with the right distance.

With the fire finger continuing to direct energy inwards, the other hand then moves up above the crown of the head to the location of the Inka window. I call this the *high crown*. Continue to direct energy, or rather allow the movement of energy, as you remain connected with the Ilahinoor field.

Next, you activate the *tube of light*. Coming around to the front, and starting with the window above your partner's head, gradually bring your hands down through the receiver's aura and down to the earth. Do this slowly enough so you can feel the thickness of the aura as you move downwards. Notice if there are any gaps or holes in the field, and allow the flow of *sami* to patch these up. Continue going down into the earth until you energetically connect with the center of the planet, the heart of the earth mother.

It's like dropping an anchor from a ship. Once it touches the bottom of the sea, there is a sense of landing within the earth. The winds can blow and tides can flow but you remain strong and stable. You are able to anchor all these fields of light, stabilizing and integrating them, grounding the energy into the body.

Too often, when there is a strong activation of the head centers without a corresponding grounding, the electrical energies can be overwhelming to the nervous system, creating a number of painful and debilitating symptoms. Balancing cosmic energies with a strong grounding is essential for opening the body to light.

The movement of *sami* through the physical body is referred to as kundalini. There are two kundalini flows. When people talk about kundalini awakening, they are usually speaking of the earth kundalini, which rises up from the root towards the crown of the head. Unless you are emotionally clear, this flow of kundalini initiates a deep release of *hucha*, which can sometimes be frightening and uncomfortable.

As awakening kundalini moves through the root chakra it brings up instinctive fears and issues around survival. As it moves through the sacral chakra it brings up issues around sexuality and intimacy. As it moves through the solar plexus it brings up issues around power and control. Only then is it able to move up through the heart and upper chakras.

All this can be very fearful and confronting for the personal ego, evoking resistance in the form of physical symptoms. This is why so many traditions speak of kundalini activation as being dangerous or painful.

In the Ilahinoor work, however, we are working primarily with the cosmic kundalini, which begins with energizing the upper chakras and restructuring your sense of personal identity. You are no longer locked into stories of victimhood and trauma, you no longer see yourself as separate from the world. Thus, when the kundalini begins to move through the same *hucha* held in the lower chakras, it can be cleared quickly and comfortably.

And then, finally, after grounding the tube of light deep into the earth, we will complete the treatment by activating the merkaba. This activation can feel very blissful and expansive, as life energies flowing through the physical body unify with the subtle and causal bodies.

PRACTICE – A COMPLETE ILAHINOOR SEQUENCE

1. Find a partner, decide who goes first.

2. Imagine the bubble of light around you. Open the window at the top of this bubble, and feel the electrical and magnetic streams of light moving simultaneously through the entire wasi, opening doorways between the upper, middle and lower worlds.

3. Invoking the Ilahinoor field, gaze into your partner's eyes for a few minutes in order to establish a deeper soul merge.

4. Activate the Ilahinoor bridge. Coming over to either side of your partner, place one hand at the ilahinoor points at the back of the head, with the other hand covering the forehead and crown. Wait for a pulsing to let you know the connection has been made.

5. Continue down step by step to connect with front and back of the heart, and then front and back of the belly.

6. Activate the whale chakra now, using the pinkie, or fire finger as a focus for laser-like divine energy. The pinkie is held a couple centimeters away from the third eye, while the whale chakra is located about 20 or 30 cm behind the back of the head.

7. Proceed from the whale chakra to the high crown, about half a meter above the head, while the fire finger continues to focus a laser like beam of light towards the third eye.

8. Standing in front of your partner and starting with the high crown, allow your hands to move down through the tube of light all the way to the center of the earth.

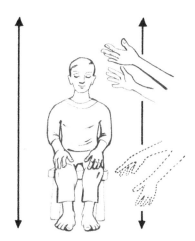

9. Activate the merkaba using the triple breath.

Allow as much time to integrate as needed. Be aware that the receiver can be in a very altered state of consciousness during this time.

CHAPTER 16
CENTERS OF IDENTITY

We have spoken earlier about the causal, subtle and physical bodies, and how they relate to each other. We will now amplify these teachings somewhat, as we examine the yogic understanding of the five *mayakoshas*, sometimes simply referred to as *koshas*.

A *mayakosha* means 'created body', distinguishing these from the Self, which is uncreated and eternal.

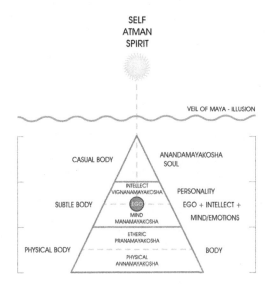

For the seers and yogis of ancient India, creation is a very orderly and systematic process. The Self exists eternally beyond the created worlds but also permeates the worlds of creation. The entire universe is a mere speck of dust within the Self. It is not separate from the Self but draws its existence from the Self.

All that can be said about the Self is *sat-chid-ananda*. It is a primordial field that permeates all things, defined through the qualities of existence, consciousness and endlessness. Some people have defined *ananda* as bliss, but it is more accurately translated as endlessness.

Creation happens through a principle known as *maya*, where the illusion of time, space and substance is imposed over the Self. The idea of a *big bang*, an entire universe being created out of nothing, is a crude version of *maya*. The universe did not emerge from nothing; there never was *nothing*. The Self is more accurately defined as *fullness*, containing all potential worlds.

"This is fullness, That is fullness," says the Isha Upanishad. "Take away fullness from fullness and fullness still remains."

The fullness of the universe emerges from the fullness of the Self, leaving the Self intact. The Self exists independent of the universe but the universe could never exist independent of the Self.

The universe is like a string of pearls, say the ancient seers of India. Each pearl reflects every pearl, each pearl contains every pearl, and each pearl is every pearl, because this pearl is the Self. You cannot separate creation from the Self, even though the human mind tends to perceive reality through this illusion of separation.

Plasma cosmologists are beginning to understand that matter is 99.999 percent plasma, and that the three states of physical matter derive from this. Plasma itself derives from the interaction between primal electric and magnetic fields that permeate the entire universe. We could say that these fields are the universe, Self expressed within creation through the projective principle of *maya*.

Likewise, quantum theory tells us that the same infinite space that extends beyond matter is also found within the heart of all matter. Matter has no physical reality of its own, independent of the primordial Self.

Thus the term *mayakosha* refers to bodies created out of primordial Self in order to reflect and express the Self within the grand illusion of space and time, a matrix we refer to as the *universe.*

Our essential identity, whether we are talking about humans, planetary systems or galactic filaments, IS this primordial Self, each expressed through five bodies in time and space, the *mayakoshas.*

The mayakoshas are subdivisions of the three bodies we looked at earlier. The *anandamayakosha,* or body of bliss, is equivalent to the causal body. The *vignanamayakosha,* or wisdom body, and the *manamayakosha,* the feeling body, are both included within the subtle body. The *pranamayakosha,* the etheric blueprint, and the *annamayakosha,* or food body, are aspects of the physical body.

These five bodies each have a distinct presence within the aura, but also have the ability to merge with each other. The merging of these bodies is the basis of merkaba teachings found in the Egyptian, Tibetan, and other esoteric traditions, in which an adept eventually manages to transmute the physical body into an immortal body of light.

Some of you may be familiar with that movie, *Lucy.* I won't detail the story here, but it's about a woman who starts to open up to more and more of her brain's potential, from the normal five or ten percent, out to twenty, thirty, fifty, eventually out to a hundred percent. And as this happens, she goes through multiple transformations within her psyche, and within her senses, seeing things in their primordial essence. As she reaches hundred percent she transforms into light, the same conscious, intelligent light that moves through all things, inseparable from everything else.

Biological evolution, as we have experienced it over long eons, represents a journey where Gaia herself is attempting to merge these five bodies on a planetary level. The basic building blocks for this process are DNA sequences, influenced by a cosmic intelligence operating through fields of light extending through vast galactic space. At certain times in our planet's history, typically during magnetic reversals, these cosmic *morphogenetic* fields imprint our cellular DNA, greatly speeding up the evolutionary process.

In *Earth Under Fire*, Paul LaViolette refers to galactic superwaves, composed of cosmic and gamma rays, periodically emanating from the center of our galaxy, preparing to move through our solar system. In his book, *Source Field Investigations*, David Wilcock explains how DNA does not require a physical medium in order to be transmitted. It can travel across vast distances riding on photons of light. Is this part of the mechanism of new creation?

We stand here in this moment of time, awaiting the birth of a new species of humanity with senses and capabilities never before seen. Sri Aurobindo referred to a supramental descent initiating this process now, which will eventually give rise to a divine human species. The Mayas referred to this next species as *homo luminous.*

PRACTICE – SHIFTING IDENTITIES

1. Take a few minutes to do an Ilahinoor self-treatment.

2. As you achieve an expanded state of consciousness, you will now move your attention to different centers of identity.

3. Start with becoming aware of the center of identity located in the subtle body. This is the middle self, the sense of who you are based on a continuity of thoughts, feelings and memories. Affirm, "I am the personal ego."

4. Go deeper into the sensations within your physical body now. As you pay attention to the flow of sensations you become aware of a cellular intelligence held within the body. It may take some time to become aware of this. It is a devic intelligence, belonging to the elemental worlds. You can learn to communicate with it by sending thoughts of appreciation. Affirm, "I am the body."

5. Allow yourself to expand out through the merkaba. Become aware of an identity held within the causal body that transcends any single incarnation, that travels from lifetime to lifetime, and is not bound by time. Affirm, "I am the soul".

6. Now become aware that all these levels of identity, although distinct from each other, are relatively impermanent. Allow your merkaba to extend out beyond the boundaries of time and space. Your deepest identity IS the Self that permeates all Creation, and extends beyond Creation. There are no thoughts, feelings or qualities associated with this state, just a sense of Presence underlying all these mayakoshas. Dissolve into the knowing, "I AM."

CHAPTER 17
ILAHINOOR DIAGONAL TREATMENT

In the ayurvedic tradition, there are three kinds of energy flows that can be utilized for healing: vertical, horizontal and diagonal. Of these, the diagonal flows, which stimulate the flow of kundalini moving through the spine, are the most powerful.

There are diagonal flows that move through all the major joints, and as they do so, bring deep healing into the skeletal structures of the body. These joints include the neck, shoulders, elbows, wrists, hips, knees and ankles.

A sample treatment connecting energies between these thirteen joints would include the following:

- Back of neck and left elbow
- Left elbow and right wrist
- Back of neck and right elbow
- Right elbow and left wrist
- Both wrists together to balance right and left
- Right shoulder and left hip
- Left hip and right knee
- Right knee and left ankle

- Left ankle and right wrist
- Left shoulder and right hip
- Right hip and left knee
- Left knee and right ankle
- Right ankle and left wrist
- Both ankles together to ground the energy

PRACTICE – DIAGONAL FLOWS

This treatment can be done with a partner, but with a little bit of ingenuity, can also be performed on your own. If you are

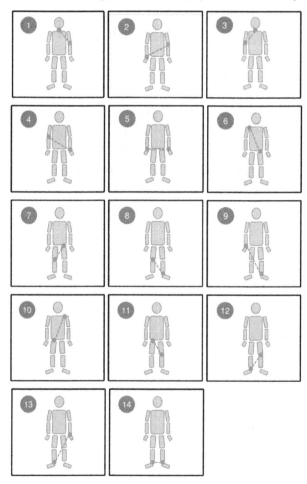

working with a partner, it is easiest sitting on chairs facing each other, although this treatment can also be done with the receiver lying down face up on a massage table.

Note that there are positions where you are connecting the ankles with opposite wrists. These are especially important in terms of Chinese meridian theory. Known as the four gates, all the meridian flows move through these joints, so holding points of contact helps in quickly balancing all the meridian flows.

1. Start with activating the flow of electrical and magnetic streams of sami by opening the window on top of the bubble.

2. Invoke the Ilahinoor field while creating a soul merge through the eyes.

3. Activate the Ilahinoor bridge, then continue down to connect with the heart and belly centers.

4. Starting with the back of the neck, use your hands to alternately move down through the joints in the order described above. Maintain each position long enough to feel the energy pulsing between the diagonal points of contact.

5. Activate the whale chakra and the high crown.

6. Move your hands through the tube of light from high crown down to the center of the earth.

7. Activate the merkaba.

EXTENDED DIAGONAL FLOWS

Once you have learned this basic diagonal sequence you can also add a few additional areas in the body, such as the jaws, lymph nodes, liver and spleen. A sample sequence could include:

- Back of neck with right jaw
- Right jaw with left shoulder
- Left shoulder with lymph nodes under right arm
- Right underarm with spleen area
- Spleen with right hip
- Right hip with left knee

- Left knee with right ankle
- Right ankle with left elbow
- Right ankle with left wrist
- Both wrists together
- Back of neck with left jaw
- Left jaw with right shoulder
- Right shoulder with lymph nodes under left arm
- Left underarm with liver area
- Liver with left hip
- Left hip with right knee
- Right knee with left ankle
- Left ankle with right elbow
- Left ankle with right wrist
- Both ankles together

PRACTICE – EXTENDED DIAGONAL FLOWS

This treatment can be done with a partner, but can also be performed on your own. If you are working with a partner, it is easiest sitting on chairs facing each other, although this treatment can also be done with the receiver lying down face up on a massage table.

Note that along with the four gates as in the previous practice, many of the diagonal flows in this extended treatment pass through specific chakras, energizing them accordingly. So for instance, the contact between jaw and opposite shoulder passes through the throat chakra, the contact between shoulder and opposite lymph region passes through the heart chakra, the contact between the lymph node and the opposite liver/spleen passes through the solar plexus, the contact between liver/spleen and opposite hip passes through the sacral chakra, and the contact between hip and opposite knee passes through the root chakra.

Ilahinoor Diagonal Treatment

1. Start with activating the flow of electrical and magnetic streams of sami by opening the window on top of the bubble.

2. Invoke the Ilahinoor field while creating a soul merge through the eyes.

3. Activate the Ilahinoor bridge, then continue down to include the heart and belly centers.

4. Starting with the back of the neck, use your hands to alternately move down through the joints in the order described above. Maintain each position long enough to feel the energy pulsing between the diagonal points of contact.

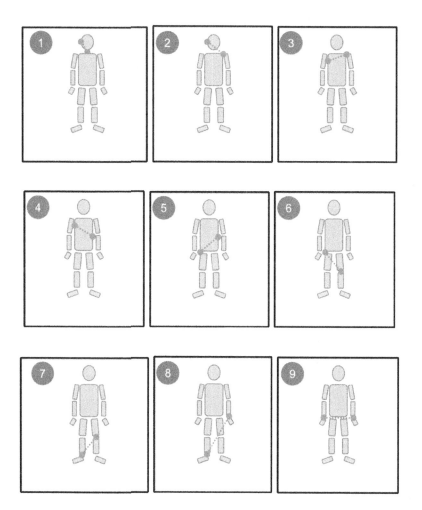

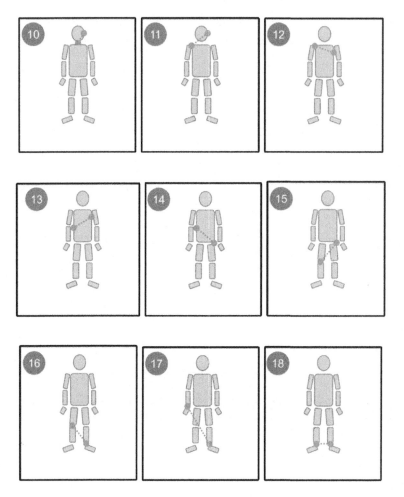

5. Activate the whale chakra and the high crown.

6. Move your hands through the tube of light from high crown down to the center of the earth.

7. Activate the merkaba.

CHAPTER 18
SPINAL TREATMENT

The spine is the foundation of the human energy system. There are three kundalini channels moving alongside the spine, the *sushumna* channel which runs through the center of the vertebral column, and twin channels known as the *ida* and *pingala*, which move along the spine like a double helix, criss-crossing at each chakra.

The flexibility and openness of the spine reflects the health of the entire body. There are spinal nerves that connect with every organ system, and the cerebrospinal fluid that moves through the vertebral column between cranium and sacrum, is an indicator for mental, emotional and physical stability.

Thus, including the spine in any Ilahinoor treatment can be very useful. It can be as simple as simply connecting with each vertebra of the spine, and gently manipulating it while bringing the Ilahinoor energy through. You could also experiment with placing your hands in different regions of the spine, and applying a light vibratory pressure.

PRACTICE – SPINAL TREATMENT

This practice can be done with receiver seated backwards on a chair so that the spine is exposed. It can also be done with the receiver lying face down on a massage table. Unless you happen to be a contortionist, a self treatment may be rather more difficult.

1. Start with opening the doorway between the worlds.

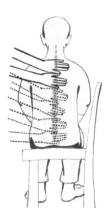

2. Do the basic soul merge, while invoking the Ilahinoor field

3. Activate the Ilahinoor bridge, then move down to include the heart and belly.

4. With one hand at the top of the receiver's head, the fingers of the other hand move down the spinal column, one vertebra at a time, making firm but gentle contact. Remaining one or two breaths in each position, you very gently press on the vertebra towards the left, towards the right, and then in towards the center. Starting with the atlas joint, you proceed one vertebra at a time down to the coccyx, or tailbone.

5. Then placing both hands over the upper back, gently vibrate the entire region for a few seconds, then stop abruptly, holding the point of contact while you feel an activation of energy. Do the same for the middle back and the lower back.

6. Focus especially on areas of the back where the receiver might be experiencing inflammation, pain, or discomfort.

7. Then continue on to activate the whale chakra, and then the high crown.

8. Move your hands slowly down the tube of light, anchoring the Ilahinoor field down into the earth.

9. End with the three-breath merkaba activation.

CHAPTER 19
MISCELLANEOUS
TREATMENTS

There are no specific rules in this work, except to simply follow your intuitive guidance. This book includes guidelines, but there are no strict rules, and once learned, this work can be effectively combined with a number of healing traditions, including Reiki, Reconnective Healing, Quantum Touch, Pranic Healing, Polarity Therapy, Matrix Energetics, and Acupressure.

Much of healing is about unifying the different bodies, so that life energy can flow easily and gracefully between them. The physical body is animated by the prana body, which in turn is influenced by the emotional and mental bodies, which in turn are guided and inspired by the causal body. When there is no hucha, there is no resistance to the flow of life energy, and the body can respond to immense healing forces beyond itself.

I have seen all sorts of spontaneous healings happen during this work. Ilahinoor is also useful for people experiencing physical or psychological addictions, as well as for those who are making a transition between worlds.

Below is a sample of other healing treatments:

PRACTICE – SIMULTANEOUS TREATMENT

In this treatment, the two partners work on each other simultaneously.

Sitting close together, both lean forward until their foreheads touch at the third eye.

Each places one finger of each hand on the Ilahinoor points of the other person.

This position can create a very powerful connection between the two partners, and is especially beautiful when there is already closeness between the two. It can be very healing for a couple who happen to find themselves in the middle of an emotional conflict.

PRACTICE – CROWN ADJUSTMENT

Place your hand in a blessing position over the receiver's head, either physically touching or held slightly away from the body. Invoke the Ilahinoor field, and feel a downpour of light entering through the crown chakra. Experiment with subtle movements to adjust this download as needed.

PRACTICE – FOOT TREATMENT

For someone whose kundalini is already active, a good way of grounding and integrating the energy is for the giver to hold the bottoms of the receiver's feet, inviting the cosmic light in through the crown of the receiver, and magnetically attracting it all the way down the body to the soles of his or her feet.

Then reverse the flow, feeling energy from the Earth below pouring in through the soles of the feet, filling the body and moving up to the head.

Remain in this position for twenty or thirty minutes, or until the energy feels fully grounded and balanced. This treatment can also be very powerful for someone who is tired, stressed, or experiencing a kundalini overload.

PRACTICE – OFF THE BODY TREATMENT

With practice, distinguishing various layers within the energy field of the receiver becomes easy. For example, the etheric double extends a few centimeters out from the physical body, while the emotional body extends approximately one meter out beyond the skin. The mental body may extend two or three meters out, and various layers of the causal body may extend out much further.

In this treatment, the practitioner remains standing above the receiver, who is lying comfortably at ground level. Work with these energy fields as intuitively guided, using the hands to connect with the subtle fields and harmonizing them. You may find yourself moving further and further away from the physical body as you harmonize subtler and subtler layers of the field.

It is recommended that you do the basic Ilahinoor treatment a few times before attempting this more advanced treatment.

PRACTICE – PROXY TREATMENT

If the intended receiver is not physically present, someone who is physically present can serve as a proxy for that person. Working on the proxy, the practitioner no only helps the proxy but also allows this divine light to be transmitted very effectively across a physical distance to the person for whom it is intended. This treatment can be especially helpful if a strong positive connection exists between the receiver and the proxy.

PRACTICE – GROUP TREATMENT

This method is one of my favorite ways of working with the Ilahinoor field. One person lies down on a massage table or a comfortable mat, with several others making a circle around the receiver, holding different positions on the body. It helps to have one person cradling the head, and another grounding the feet. Include the chakras and joints, and any specific problem areas. Feel free to move around the body as intuitively guided. Use diagonal contacts across the body if you wish.

The receiver states his or her intention for the healing, and the circle responds by invoking the Ilahinoor field to support this intention. At the end of the treatment, the givers slowly lift their hands away from the physical body, giving the receiver a couple of minutes to integrate. Group members then rotate positions around the circle so that everyone gets a turn at each position.

PRACTICE – CIRCLE HEALING

This is a simple and playful way to share the Ilahinoor energy with a group of people. Everybody stands in a circle, and then makes a half turn so they are all facing in the same direction. Place your hands on the person in front of you while receiving a blessing from the person behind you.

PRACTICE – GAZING CIRCLE

Here the intent is simply to sit within a circle of people and call in the Ilahinoor field, with each participant holding eye contact with one other participant for as long as feels right. Either participant within a partnership may break eye contact whenever desired, go within to integrate for a moment, and then move on to another participant in the circle. This is a powerful exercise for quickly entering into deep states of joyful, unified consciousness.

PRACTICE – GROUP SOUL TREATMENT

This is an amazingly powerful transmission of light that happens by simply attuning with the group soul of any group of people gathered together with focused intention. The same chakra system that is activated by the Ilahinoor field for an individual can be activated on the level of the group soul. When the crown heart, and earth chakras of a group are activated in his way, the energies can flow very profoundly through the entire group without the need for individual physical transmissions.

This treatment is more advanced, and requires the practitioner to have developed a certain degree of unification within the subtle bodies, and to be able to withstand large amounts of divine light channeling through the body.

PRACTICE – HIGHER DIMENSIONAL TRANSMISSIONS

Once you have learned to work with the Ilahinoor field, and your access to he high self is established, giving an Ilahinoor session becomes even simpler. You simply make a clear request to the *aumakua* and then let it go, allowing the transmission to happen by itself.

I first recognized the possibilities of this when I was asked to do a long distance healing, promised to do so, and then forgot. To my surprise, the person called me up the next day thanking me for what she described as a very profound experience.

When the same thing happened on a couple of other occasions I realized that soul intention comes from a different place than mental intention. As our physical bodies become increasingly merged with our subtle bodies, our intentions become a gate through which higher dimensional energies can flow directly from the source field to whichever persons or situations our attention is directed towards. The more connected I AM with my inner being, the more this unified light can flow wherever it chooses to go, blessing each other and our planet in accordance with a higher evolutionary plan!

PRACTICE – ILAHINOOR FOR BIRTHING AND DYING

Ilahinoor helps to open the doorway between worlds. As such, it can be a beautiful experience for everyone involved to hold this space of unified light as a loved one makes a passage from one dimensional state to another, whether in birth or in death. It can also be useful to assist someone who is making a shamanic journey by holding him in this state of expanded unified awareness!

I was halfway across the world when my father died of heart failure. The night before his passage, I had been relaxing at a friend's home when I felt an enormous light flooding my entire body, filling me with a deep sense of peace and ecstasy. I felt somehow that this feeling had to do with my father, even though I had no inkling of his impending heart attack. When my brother called me with the news the following morning, I was shocked and saddened, but not surprised. I had felt the night before that he was ready to go and that he was being guided smoothly and joyfully into the light.

PRACTICE – ILAHINOOR MUSIC

My friend Denean has created a beautiful CD, *Gaia's Prayer*, which includes some Ilahinoor chants as well as whale music. It is available through Cdbaby.com.

CHAPTER 20
GAIANOOR

Even though it seems that we have worked hard to destroy the very foundation of our existence, this Earth is still our home, and She still sees us as her children. Our species has evolved as part of an experiment to weave creator consciousness into the heart of matter. Perhaps the experiment has not worked as well as it might, but it is not over yet. We are a species in transition, and a greater dawn is at hand.

In May 2016, while on retreat in the magnificent Black Sea region of Turkey, I took some time to go into a shamanic space, communing with the heart of the Earth and the power of the Sky. I felt myself entering the primordial space before the existence of time, creator dreaming a new dream, Gaia emerging from the dream in a beautiful wild dance of creation.

It was a beautiful experience. I felt the mighty forces of Gaia moving up through my feet, and felt we approaching the dawn of a new age. The Inkas talk about the pachakuti, and the return of light as we approach the Sixth Sun. The rishis of ancient India speak about the dawn of Satya Yuga, the age of light. Sri Aurobindo speaks of the next human species emerging in response to the descent of supramental light.

I had always felt that Ilahinoor was an expression of this supramental light. I felt it was connected in some way with the approach of the galactic superwave that Paul LaViolette refers to.

But if Ilahinoor represented the descent of a cosmic light, what was the response from Gaia? In the Inka work I had become aware of the principle of ayni, and how the downward flow of electrical sami was immediately reciprocated by an upward flow of magnetic sami.

So now, as I placed my attention on the energy rising up through my feet, I realized this was Gaia's response to the flow of Ilahinoor moving downwards. If the intention of Ilahinoor was to anchor supramental fields of light to assist in planetary evolution, Gaia's response was to activate new DNA potentials to make this possible. As I recorded in my journal:

"From far out in the supramental realms I felt something enter her womb, a galactic seed that arced across the electric fires of Shiva's dance. I felt a mighty golden hammer break open the door of humanity's illusion, calling us to enter the deep heart of creation with Gaia, and find our way home.

"I then saw the sun-eyed children of a marvelous dawn, birthed from beyond the veils of perceived separation, bodies made beautiful by spirit's fire, shining with the power of love's desire for itself.

"I saw that seed being planted, and felt the response from Gaia. The supramental force was entering the structures of human DNA. We were entering the cocoon of this new creation. The human butterfly, the great cosmic child of a New Sun, was but a heartbeat away from manifesting fully in all forms and structures of creation.

"This was the new species awaited so long, being birthed on the other side of the magnetic reversal. It was human in form but not in expression, far removed from the anchor of separation and duality that has defined our matrix for so many eons. Its new matrix was the direct awareness of oneness that pervaded the infinite multiplicity of forms, so that the entire web of life could find its center, and radiate out further.

"This was not a human species alone, but carried the potentials of all species of life to evolve further. This was indeed the birth of a New Earth consciousness: not just homo luminous, but Gaia luminous, a planetary web of living light. I became Gaia then, and felt the mighty waves of delight that rippled through her being, as the dance of Shiva was once again renewed in a brand new creation.

"I saw that the old world with its systems of soulless greed, mindless fear, and heartless oppression will very quickly fall away. There is no vital force sustaining these structures anymore. And the seeds of the New Earth are germinating just as quickly within the hearts of all who choose to awaken now.

"The dreamer awakens from his dream, and all creation explodes with joy."

PRACTICE – GAIANOOR

I describe this practice for working with a partner. It can be modified accordingly when working on yourself.

1. Start with activating the Inka flows by opening the window above the crown.

2. Invoke the Ilahinoor field as you establish soul contact with your partner. As you gaze into each other's eyes, you are looking beyond the physical eyes to the wide space of infinity beyond.

3. Activate the Ilahinoor bridge, and then continue to connect heart and belly, waiting for the pulse to let you know when you are ready to move on.

4. Activate the whale chakra, pointing the fire finger (pinkie) into the third eye while the other hand is held at the location of the whale chakra 20 to 30 cm behind the back of the head.

5. With the pinkie still in place, move the other hand to the location of the Inka window above the crown of the head, activating the high crown.

6. Bring your hands down through the tube of light, starting with the high crown, and eventually anchoring deep inside the earth.

7. Now become aware of a return stream of conscious intention in response to Ilahinoor. This is the Gaianoor frequency, moving up through your partner's feet into the region of the perineum. You can assist this flow by allowing the Gaianoor to come up through your feet and up your own body, then focusing it out through your third eye towards the perineal region of your partner.

8. Imagine going back to a moment in time shortly after conception, back to when the first eight cells were still

undifferentiated. This field of psychic memory is still held within the perineum, and can be easily programmed with new information.

9. As the Gaianoor frequency enters this eight-cell matrix, imagine the DNA within these cells going through a metamorphosis, responding to Gaia's intent for birthing a new human species. Wait until you feel this shift taking place.

10. Activate the three-breath merkaba, this time feeling the tube torus extending out from the perineum and flooding the entire body with new biological codes.

CHAPTER 21
INKA ENERGY SYSTEM

Lets' go back to the Inka practices. Their understanding of the energy bodies reflected their belief that all things are connected, and therefore it is possible to communicate with all things. They felt that all things are connected in the flow of *sami*, and therefore there is no hierarchy in the universe. They saw that everything in the universe is alive, and therefore must be treated with respect.

Each ancient culture has evolved its own understanding of human energy based on their underlying perceptions and beliefs about reality. For example, the Chinese culture was focused on the mastery of life energies, and so developed rituals for healing as well as combat based on an understanding of *chi*. The Indian culture was focused on unifying the life energies, and hence developed yogic practices for raising the *kundalini shakti* and experiencing cosmic consciousness.

The Inka culture was focused on *ayni*, the reciprocal balance between all things, and so developed strategies for transmuting *hucha* into *sami*. Whereas the Chinese traditions tended to emphasize the earth polarity, and Indian traditions tended to emphasize the cosmic polarity, the Inka tradition emphasized the inseparable connection between earth and sky.

The Chinese understood that *chi* circulates through a network of *meridians* and *psychic channels*. The Indians spoke of *kundalini* moving through a series of *chakras* and *nadis*. The Inkas refer to *kausay* circulating between earth and sky aided by the *nawis* and *chumpas*.

Nawi means eye. There are seven eyes used by the soul to perceive subtle realities. While there are similarities between these *nawis* and the *chakras*, there are also significant differences.

The *nawis* are represented as cones rather than as wheels, each of the cones facing either front or back. The equivalent of the root chakra is called the *siki nawi,* a cone with its eye facing the back.

The equivalent of the sacral chakra is the *qosqo nawi,* with its eye facing the front. *Qosqo* means center. Just as with the Chinese understanding of the *tan tien,* or the Japanese understanding of the *hara,* the Inkas recognized the qosqo nawi as the center of the life force within the body. The capital of the Inka empire was Cusco, which also means *center.*

The next one up is the *sonqo nawi,* equivalent to the heart, again facing the front. The *kunka nawi* is at the throat, and the *qanchis nawi* is the spiritual eye, each of these also facing the front. They also count the two physical eyes as part of the energy system, the left eye known as *lloqe,* and the right eye known as *panya.*

Qanchis actually means seventh. The Hindus talk about this center as the third eye, but to them it's the seventh eye. Why so? If you count the nawis, starting with the siki nawi, qosqo nawi, sonqo nawi, kunka nawi, lloqe nawi, pana nawi, and qanchis nawi, that makes seven.

Although not traditionally associated as such, I also include the window above the energy bubble as a nawi, which would be the equivalent of the crown chakra. Since the bubble, or luminous egg, is known as the *poqpo,* I call this this the *poqpo nawi,* and it faces above. The bubble itself completely encloses the physical body, incorporating the *pranamaya kosha,* or the energy body.

If you were paying attention, you may have noticed that the solar plexus is not included as a nawi. Why is that? The solar plexus is not an eye. Rather, this is where the seed of enlightenment, the *inka muyu,* is located. This is the famed solar

THE NAWIS

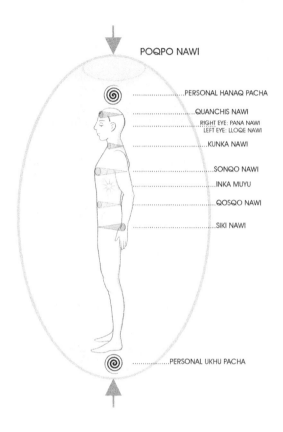

POQPO NAWI

PERSONAL HANAQ PACHA

QUANCHIS NAWI

RIGHT EYE: PANA NAWI
LEFT EYE: LLOQE NAWI

KUNKA NAWI

SONQO NAWI

INKA MUYU

QOSQO NAWI

SIKI NAWI

PERSONAL UKHU PACHA

disk of the Inkas. Many of the practices are about gradually awakening this seed, and activating the solar disk.

When the Spanish conquistadores arrived in South America, they had heard tales about the solar disk, the treasure of all treasures, and went hunting for it, slaughtering many in the process. For a culture that had no concept of multi-dimensional realities, anything precious could only be associated with gold, and they could not perceive that it was an internal treasure.

However, for those who seek this treasure and are able to find it, it manifests as serenity, radiance and personal power.

The Inka muyu is associated with the tree of life. If we go back to the Genesis story, there were two trees in the Garden of Eden. The first tree was the knowledge of good and evil, the experience of duality. The second tree was the tree of life, the return to unity. The *paqos* taught that when the *inka muyu* is awakened, it creates a tree of life within the energy bodies, and opens the doorways to unity. There are beautiful Inka practices for reconnecting with the tree of life, which we will explore later.

PRACTICE – THE TWO TREES

Western culture has been heavily conditioned by the Genesis myth, where God created the first man and woman and placed them in the Garden of Eden, inviting them to eat of any fruit they wished, except from the tree of knowledge, which would open their eyes to good and evil.

Why this prohibition? Take some time to contemplate this. What does this tree symbolize in your own life, and in our current global culture? How does eating the fruit of this tree reflect in our relationship with each other, with our planet, with ourselves? What does the serpent in the garden represent? Why did he approach Eve rather than Adam? What is the nature of *sin*?

The Inka culture, on the other hand, has been conditioned to seek the tree of life, the awareness of an underlying unity between all things. What does this tree symbolize in your own life, and in our current global culture? How would eating the fruit of this tree affect our relationship with each other, with our planet, with ourselves?

The anaconda is seen as the guardian of this tree of life. Could this be the same serpent that 'tempted' Eve? What is its true function and role in our lives? Why is kundalini energy also represented in the form of a serpent? In the yogic tradition, the kundalini energies are represented as two spirals of life energy ascending through the spine. How are these related to the double helix within our DNA?

Albert Einstein was once asked what was the most important question in his life. "Is the universe friendly?" he responded. How can we reinvent the Genesis Story so it can serve the next phase of our evolutionary journey? How can we move out from victimhood, fear and limitation to experiencing the infinite goodness of a friendly universe?

CHAPTER 22
THE SIKI NAWI

We will begin now to work with the nawis, one by one. Let's start with the siki nawi. The siki nawi is the root center, our connection with Mother Earth, or Pachamama. As you notice in the chart, the eye of the siki nawi faces the back, and is the only nawi structured that way. Why is that?

It is literally like a tail, and has a deep sensitivity to the earth. It represents our connection with the earth through the tail. Most indigenous cultures have a disdain for furniture or chairs. They simply squat on the earth. Whether waiting for a bus, or birthing a baby, or hanging out with companions, or eating their meals, they are either squatting or sitting cross legged directly on the earth.

The energy is open. I hear some people talk about 'earthing', as if it was a new concept. For indigenous people it is a way of life. They walk barefoot, they squat on the earth, they spend time absorbing *prana* from nature, and they remain healthy. They don't have the nervous system disorders and neuroses that people suffer when they have lost touch with the earth.

Many are starting to recognize that most of our work environments do not support us. Confined in air-conditioned rooms, sitting for 8 hours a day, is cutting us off from the source of life, draining our life force. How do we counteract this?

The siki nawi is always connected to the earth, whether physically or energetically. When we lose touch with the earth physically we can maintain the energetic connection. The Taoist tradition refers to the *microcosmic orbit,* a continuous flow of prana, or chi, that moves up the back and down the front, and simultaneously up the front and down the back.

When the siki nawi is connected with the earth these flows become very open and continuous. These flows originate from the earth. The siki nawi is your connection with the earth, and also the generator for these flows within the body.

When you are connected with this nawi you are connected with the earth and the intelligence of the earth. What happens if a dog is lost in the forest? It will circle around until it finds its track. How do whales navigate, how do butterflies and birds travel vast distances across the skies on their migration patterns? It's by connecting with the magnetic currents of the earth through the siki nawi, and listening. It's the same thing with Australian aboriginals following the song lines to traverse continents.

The siki nawi is an instinctive center. It has to do with the cellular mind. You know without knowing how you know. You simply trust that knowing, and follow that knowing. When the tsunami came in 2004, animals and tribal people were up in the mountains when the waves came. They knew they had to be up high without knowing how they knew. This is what the instinctive center is about.

When the planes hit the twin towers in September 2001, there were many people who woke up that morning and couldn't bring themselves to go to work that day. They weren't there when those buildings came down. I've talked with people who felt they weren't supposed to travel on a certain day, only to find out later that their ship, or their plane went down.

So what was happening? They were following their instincts, and this is something we can all develop. For the Q'ero, people this also had to do with not having masks. The more we put on a mask, or pretend, the less we can stay connected with the siki nawi. Being transparently open in simplicity and truth is what keeps the siki nawi functional and strong.

Supposing you are standing at the edge of a waterfall, asking yourself if it's safe to jump. Sometimes there is just conditioned fear. We need to distinguish between this and the siki nawi. When the siki nawi is saying no, it is a specific sensation. Maybe there is a rock I cannot see, or the water isn't deep enough, or whatever. If you can learn to distinguish the warnings of the siki nawi from conditioned fear, you can take risks in life, knowing that you will be safe.

Children growing up to trust the siki nawi don't need to be supervised all the time. They go out and play in the jungle, or jump across streams and puddles, and their parents don't need to be constantly afraid they're going to drown or be stung by a rattlesnake. They have learned to trust their instinctive knowing, and don't experience themselves as separate from the earth. Conversely, a mother's fear and anxiety about her children can often create a field where they become disconnected from the siki nawi. And then of course they can trip over their own feet and hurt themselves.

As we learn to listen to the siki nawi, we arrive at an absolute fearlessness of mind. You develop a living relationship with the Earth, which leads to an absolute trust that you are here on her invitation, and that you are being taken care of. Where there is trust there cannot be fear. Where there is trust, there is a willingness to surrender to the natural flow of creation. Where there is trust you feel safe, knowing you are not a victim, but a co-creator with life.

Enlightenment for the Inkas is simply about trusting the flow rather than resisting it. What is suffering? It's either being attached to an outcome, or resisting this flow. When the three worlds are connected together, and when your connection with Mother Earth is strong, you experience a spontaneity of being, without judgments, comparisons, resistance, or fear. It becomes a way of life.

The following practice refers to opening the vertebral column to the flow of sami.

PRACTICE – SAYWA TAQE

It's easier to first do this practice with a partner, although it can be easily done on your own as well.

1. Stand back to back with a partner. You're not touching, just slightly apart. Imagine that the energy starts being generated at the siki nawi, goes up the back for one person (decide which one), jumps from crown to crown, and then comes down the back for the other person, jumping from siki nawi to siki nawi to complete the loop.

2. Start the circulation from the siki nawi, and let it move faster and faster until it's a strong continuous flow. Don't try and follow the circulation of energy with your mind or direct it with your breath. It is up to the cellular mind to generate this, and is typically much faster than the mind can follow.

3. Slow it down... stop… reverse directions.

4. How does that feel? Are you able to experience the current? Do you feel it coming up from the earth? If you don't feel this circulation as strongly as you would like, open the window wider, and focus on the magnetic stream flowing up from the Earth. It is this magnetic force that generates the circulation of energy from the siki nawi.

5. In the Taoist tradition there are two flows, one is up the back and down the front, and the other is up the front and down the back. Notice which one is easier.

6. The earth kundalini generally flows up the back. But in the ilahinoor work we are also encouraging the downward cosmic flow. You are learning to harmonize the flows so they are both equally strong.

CHAPTER 23
THE QOSQO NAWI

B eing able to transmute energy is the beginning of mastery. The Inkas did not see the world in terms of duality, but as kausay pacha, an ocean of energy that was constantly in movement. There were no fixed ideas of good and evil, except as it related to the natural flow of life. Being attuned to the flow was good, and created harmony and joy. Resisting the flow was bad, since that created fear and suffering.

Resistance to the flow created heaviness, or *hucha*, which not only separated us from the natural flow of life, but created immense suffering based on false identification with the drop rather than this vast ocean. Yet, *hucha* was not real in itself, and could be easily transmuted with proper awareness and understanding.

How is this done? Although conscious awareness of dysfunctional patterns may be useful, this is not usually enough in itself to produce deep transformation. However, there is a way we can do this energetically that is simple, effective and fun, and this is where the qosqo nawi comes in.

How many of you are deeply sensitive to other people's energies, often picking up their emotional or psychic 'stuff', and getting overwhelmed as a result? This tends to be especially true of therapists, healers, or activists, especially when confronting issues around violence, betrayal, trauma, abuse and victimhood.

Or how many of you have been dealing with your own deep insecurities and fears, childhood patterns around not being worthy enough, strong enough, or deserving enough? How many of us feel helpless in the face of oppression, greed and brutality so prevalent in the world? We live in a very fractured reality, and our tendency is to often shut down, get depressed, or go into denial. How can we truly help without getting bogged down in the quicksand of negativity?

When I say that the Inkas did not believe in negativity it is not a statement of denial. It is rather the ability to perceive differently and to join a deeper flow underlying all the circumstances of our lives, and therefore transform victimization into mastery.

How is this done? As long as we are operating out of the middle world, our perceptions are necessarily limited. But as soon as we connect the three worlds, our perceptions change. And as perceptions change, we gain the ability to let the ocean pour in, and transform reality itself.

This is not something that can be done on the level of rational mind. However, this transmuting ability is built into our energy system, specifically at the qosqo nawi, and we can learn how to do this very easily.

It is important to understand that we are not transforming negative energy into positive energy. We are rather transmuting the illusion that negative energy exists at all. This is a function of the cellular mind, and begins to happen as we open the doorway between the worlds. Hucha transmutes into sami, and you experience yourself in a flow that transcends the duality of positive or negative, right or wrong, good or bad. Outer events may not necessarily change, but your ability to respond, and to stay in balance, will be enhanced.

When we open the window to the upper worlds, the downward flow of sami already begins to release hucha through your own body. It is also possible to use the qosqo nawi for this, whether working on yourself or with another person. This practice is known as *hucha mikhuy*.

You first become aware of the location of the qosqo nawi, usually just below the navel and slightly inside the body. You open this eye now as wide as you can, using your hands to mimic this process of opening, if needed.

Once the qosqo nawi is open, invite hucha to enter all the way in. Notice that as long as you see hucha as something negative, there will be an instinctive resistance to inviting this in. But as you open the doorway between the worlds, the cellular mind takes over, and the transmutation becomes possible.

Once the hucha enters in, it starts to get digested into sami, and moves straight up through the body. Whatever cannot get digested continues to move down as hucha, where it is digested by Pachamama, who simply regards it as compost, and receives it with gratitude. She then sends up her sami in response.

PRACTICE – HUCHA MIKHUY (SELF)

1. Open the energy bubble, and experience the streams of sami flowing down, and then simultaneously upwards. Notice how this creates a matrix of light that permeates the entire wasi. This also opens the connection between the 3 worlds, shifting your perceptions from duality to unity.

2. As the sami moves through the wasi, it already begins to clear out hucha. For additional clearing, use your intent now to open the qosqo nawi, allowing your hands to extend out from the belly to facilitate this opening, if needed.

3. Invite hucha from anywhere in the wasi to enter inside the qosqo nawi, where it can be digested. As hucha is digested, it moves up directly as sami; anything that isn't digested continues down as hucha, where it is digested by Pachamama, and then returns up as sami.

4. Notice the clarity of mind and lightness of being as hucha is digested, and as more sami begins to flow through your energy

system. Notice any release of physical or emotional symptoms as well.

PRACTICE – HUCHA MIKHUY (WITH PARTNER)

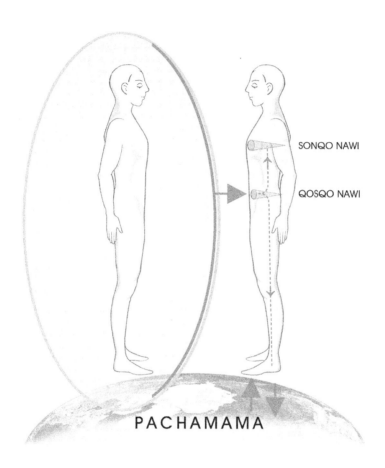

1. Open the energy bubble, and experience the streams of sami flowing down, and then simultaneously upwards. Notice how this creates a matrix of light that permeates the entire wasi. This also opens the connection between the 3 worlds, shifting your perceptions from duality to unity.

2. If your partner is familiar with the Inka work, he or she can practice the samin chakuy and saywa chakuy as well.

3. Facing your partner, use your intent now to open the qosqo nawi, allowing your hands to extend out from the belly to facilitate this opening.

4. Invite hucha from anywhere in your partner's wasi to enter inside your own qosqo nawi, where it can be digested. As hucha is digested, it moves up directly as sami; anything that isn't digested continues down as hucha, where it is digested by Pachamama, and then returns up as sami.

5. If you are sensitive, you may become aware of where in your partner's body or poqpo the hucha is being released from as it flows in towards you.

6. As sami continues to build, there will be a moment when it starts to spontaneously move out from your sonqo nawi towards your partner. Thus your partner is not only benefiting from the release of hucha, but also experiencing this transmission of sami as it flows from your heart to bless them.

7. Notice the clarity of mind and lightness of being as hucha is digested, and as more sami begins to flow through your energy system. You may find that as you digest the hucha of your partner, matching hucha within your own body also starts to get released.

8. Meanwhile, your partner is simply observing the process, noticing how they feel as their hucha is transmuted. Ultimately, there is no distinction between your hucha and their hucha. It is all simply kausay that has been blocked, and is now free to flow once again. Notice the release of physical or emotional symptoms.

PRACTICE – HUCHA MIKHUY (WITH COLLECTIVE FIELD)

Ultimately, there is no such thing as personal hucha. We are all connected through subconscious fields, and although our stories may be different, our human energy systems are essentially the same. Thus, once we learn how to digest hucha, we can also practice this with the collective field.

As you open the doorway between worlds, feel yourself expanding out through the cosmos. Open the qosqo nawi, and begin transmuting hucha from the collective field of humanity. Invite angelic beings, nature spirits, and awakened masters to join you in this great work. You are likely to experience a deep connection with Mother Earth, or Pachamama, as you assist each other in digesting collective hucha, as well as a deep opening of the heart as sami flows back out.

I find that when I am working with transmuting hucha on a collective level with Gaia, there are times when hucha flows all the way up through the crown to the galactic center, rather than downwards to the Earth. This can be a very intense transmuting process, and greatly enhances the power of the galactic waves returning back to our solar system and the earth.

CHAPTER 24
SOUL RELEASE

This next practice is something I learned to do while I was travelling through a beautiful coastal village near Rome called Terracina.

Terracina used to be a summer home for many of the popes, and is also home for the Temple of Giove going back to earlier days. Nearby is also Mount Circeo, where dwelled the siren Circe, who attempted to lure the Greek hero Ulysses, and his men, onto her rocky shores.

As I was walking through the older parts of the village, guided by friends who were hosting a workshop I was doing nearby, we passed a very interesting building, known as the Church of Purgatorio. It looked like a church, yet was adorned with a skeleton in front, holding a big banner that said, "Today it's me, tomorrow it's you."

Inside the church, holding up the dome, there were more skeletons. On the outside of the confessional boxes were skulls. Circling the walls and decorating the dome were bones in all sorts of poses, and skulls and crossbones as decorative motifs.

I was told that this church represented purgatory in the Catholic tradition, and was a holding place for souls who were not worthy enough to go to heaven yet not sinful enough to go to hell. Although such ideas don't fit into my own belief system, many around the world do believe in literal heavens and hells, which are thus projected into existence. Likewise, for those unsure about which realm they belong to, purgatories are projected into existence, where they can work out their karmas in their ultimate return to light.

This building represented one such purgatory. As I stood in front, absorbed in my own thoughts, I decided to practice a bit of hucha mikhuy on behalf of those who felt themselves trapped in this purgatory of consciousness.

I immediately felt a strong flow of hucha pouring in through my qosqo nawi. However, as it began to transmute and circulate, I realized it was not moving out through my heart as I was expecting. Rather, I felt it going straight up through the window and up to the sky.

As this continued I realized that what I was experiencing was not just hucha, but the subtle bodies of people who had been trapped in these purgatory realms, and were using this opportunity to be released into the light of their souls.

I felt the presence of mighty angelic forces assisting in this work, as thousands of people began to break out of their purgatorial prison.

I wasn't sure how long this process would take, but twenty minutes went by and it was still continuing unabated. I was supposed to meet my group in an hour to have pizza together, so I eventually decided to move on. As we started walking, dead people continued to move through my energy bodies, in through the qosqo nawi, and out through the poqpo nawi. I felt a sense of euphoria as I experienced the healing light and love pouring in from angelic forces who were assisting.

I found myself unable to walk very fast because of the power of the energies cycling through. As we walked along the promontory to eventually rejoin the rest of the group two hours later, the process was still continuing, and only stopped when I took my first bite of pizza!

PRACTICE – SOUL RELEASE

1. Tune in to someone who has died. This could be somebody you know personally, it could be the site of a natural disaster or historical battlefield, perhaps a 'haunted' house, or simply an

intention you hold for helping clear out the purgatorial worlds that extends beyond the physical body to include our subtle bodies.

2. Often these people may not even be aware that their physical bodies have died, and continue trying to fulfill their dreams, desires, addictions or agendas as when they were still in physical form. Becoming aware that they have died often comes as a shock, especially if their death has been traumatic in some way.

3. Open the energy bubble, allow sami to circulate between sky and earth as doorways between the three worlds open. Invoke the presence of angelic helpers, or dreamwalkers, to assist in the process. They delight to work with us in this way, and there is no reason for fear.

4. Open the qosqo nawi. This time, instead of inviting hucha, invite the subtle bodies of these 'dead' people to circulate through your qosqo nawi, and then up through the poqpo nawi into the realms of light. You will typically feel a great deal of love accompanying this process, and much gratitude from those who have been able to move on.

CHAPTER 25
THE SONQO NAWI

Being able to transmute energy is the beginning of mastery. Most of the time when we are leaking energy, or trying to manage our lives with a limited amount of energy, we don't have the ability to dive very deep or go very high into our multi-dimensional Self. But once we learn how to transmute hucha into sami, we have access to universal energy at all times.

When you have practiced the hucha mikhuy work long enough, the qosqo nawi will get turned on automatically as needed, followed by the opening of your heart. You will have the energy potential available to truly explore the infinite land-scapes of the upper world and lower world.

This energy potential is known as *munay*. It is the joining of compassion with the power of intention, or will. When we learn to generate munay there is nothing we are not capable of. I am reminded of Teilhard de Chardin, "Some day, after we have mastered the winds, the waves, the tides and gravity, we shall harness for God the energies of love. Then for the second time in the history of the world, we will have discovered fire."

We are often conditioned to think that we need to keep our heart open to life and to others, even if it is painful. For instance, there is a Buddhist practice known as *tonglin,* where you attempt to transmute someone else's pain by breathing it into your own heart, then breathing out love. While this is beautiful in theory, the heart is not designed to receive hucha. Its job rather is to transmit sami. We end up feeling drained and depleted because we are trying to transmute through the sonqo nawi what can only be transmuted by the qosqo nawi.

Once we get drained and overwhelmed there is an opposite tendency to close down our heart completely. Or we look for ways to protect ourselves energetically, forgetting that we need protect ourselves only if we perceive that there is something outside ourselves that can harm us. Once we learn to connect with the three worlds, we realize there is no inside or outside, no negative or positive, and nothing to protect from because I am not separate from anything else.

The transmuting of hucha into sami creates a full circle. If you are practicing hucha mikhuy with somebody, you invite their hucha into the qosqo nawi, transmute it into sami, and then send this out through the sonqo nawi. Each time you do this you feel lighter and stronger, because you are participating in a true exchange of ayni, you are generating munay.

This is the relationship that Gaia, or Pachamama, has with us. She is not identified with being a victim, and is not trapped in the world of duality. Thus, although the balance of life may be greatly affected from the rampant destruction of species and gross misuse of natural resources wreaked by humans on this planet, she herself as a planetary consciousness is untouched, and simply takes the opportunity to transmute our hucha into sami.

What a beautiful example of unconditional love!

So one of the functions of the sonqo nawi is to assist in stepping up the heavy frequencies of hucha and sending it out as sami. The heart also has another function, which in some respects is quite the opposite. This is to receive high cosmic frequencies of light, and to step them down into a frequency the body can comfortably absorb.

This is the task we face in these times. We spoke earlier about the incoming galactic superwave, composed of cosmic rays and gamma rays. For the most part, these frequencies pass right our bodies and through the earth without having a discernible effect, except perhaps on planetary weather patterns.

But what if we could harness the power of these cosmic rays and gamma rays to raise the vibrational frequency of our physical bodies? This is a mysterious process not yet fully understood, which has to do with our body's ability to hold and radiate light, a phenomenon known as bioluminescence. The yogic traditions of India and they mystery schools of ancient Egypt were designed to harness these cosmic energies and use them to immortalize the body, a process sometimes known as ascension.

This is the other function of the sonqo nawi. The two functions could well be linked. The more we learn to transmute hucha, the more we are prepared to also integrate cosmic light. You may wish to invoke the Ilahinoor field while practicing hucha mikhuy to further deepen your experience of this work.

PRACTICE – HUCHA MIKHUY HEALING CIRCLE

1. Participants sit in a circle. Each person opens up their energy bubble, allowing the downward and upward streams of light to interact, creating a subtle matrix of light that fills the entire group space.

2. Take a minute or two to invite friends and family into the circle that you would like to assist. Feel a deepening of presence as they link in. You may also take some time to invite your teachers, guides, planetary masters, nature guardians and healing angels.

3. Each person in the circle opens their qosqo nawi, inviting hucha from anywhere in the circle to be received and transmuted. As the transmutation continues, there will eventually be an overflow of sami that moves out through each heart back to the ones who have been invited. The sami flowing out from the heart is also known as munay, and can be directed for healing on whatever level is required.

4. Continue to the next step, inviting all those who have been affected by various traumas and circumstances out in the world. This could include, natural calamities, war, and civil unrest. Entire regions and human collectives could be invoked. You will often feel enormous waves of hucha coming in to be transmuted, and equally strong waves of sami returning back.

5. Finally, move on to connect with the collective consciousness of humanity, receiving this hucha and transmuting it. You will feel a deep connection with Mother Earth as she participates with you in this work, and the presence of many masters of light as they channel through you. This is a powerful hucha feast, and is a beautiful way of contributing to planetary transformation!

CHAPTER 26
THE KUNKA NAWI

We move up now to the kunka nawi, located at the throat. This is the key to expressing ourselves out in the world. When coupled with the sonqo nawi, it is the power to speak from the heart. When coupled with the qosqo nawi, it is the power to make things happen with the power of your intention. When coupled with the qanchis nawi, it is the ability to discern truth.

Just as *munay* is the energy generated by the heart, *rimay* refers to the energy generated by the throat. When joined with the other nawis, it is the ability to speak your truth freely, compassionately, spontaneously and powerfully.

One of the unfortunate casualties of our culture is truth. There is much corruption out in the world today, constant attempts to manipulate people and their perceptions of reality. The same media that denounces 'fake news' also generates it. War is packaged as peace, slavery as freedom, and ignorance as strength. Hidden agendas are at work behind most political alliances, economic manipulations, and military interventions around the world.

Where do you look for truth in the midst of all this *doublespeak*, as George Orwell terms it?

The ability to discern truth comes from being able to see the big picture. It also requires that we are willing to see clearly without hidden agendas of our own, whether based in fear, projection, or denial. Mahatma Gandhi spoke about *satyagraha*, truth force, as a means to fight slavery, ignorance and oppression. This truth force is rimay. It is the recognition that in truth is our highest freedom, and our greatest strength.

Where do we find the courage to live our truth, to face the forces of injustice, greed, and oppression so rampant in the world? Even more so, where do we find the courage to see ourselves clearly, where these same dark forces lurk in the shadows, fueled by the same unhealed fears?

I had a dream many years ago, where I found myself as a foot soldier in the Roman army. In the distance could be seen a fearsome monster, terrorizing everything in its path. The centurion was looking for a volunteer to go fight the monster. The soldiers all looked at each other, shaking in their boots, unwilling to take on the challenge.

Eventually I decided it was up to me. I told the centurion I was ready to fight, but that I would not require my sword or shield or armor. As I approached the monster, open handed, I found myself saying, "I am God's creature, and you are God's creature. There is nothing but love between us."

The monster shrunk down in size, and coming close enough, I realized it was nothing but a terrified little turkey, surrounded by mirrors and amplifiers to make it appear loud and fearsome, more afraid of me than I could ever be of him.

The power of truth is that it shrinks down our fears to where we can see ourselves as we truly are, and in that seeing, perceive the world differently as well. As judgments fall away, so do our fears. And as fear dissolves, we are no longer the powerless victims we claim to be. Rather, we become fierce and honorable defenders of truth, peaceful warriors in service to the living earth.

The following practice helps us to connect with the truth of our being, and develops our ability to communicate this with clarity, wisdom and compassion.

PRACTICE – THE POQPO TAQE

This is a partner exercise but can also be done on your own. When performed with a partner, it helps both partners to open their energy bubbles wider.

1. Face a partner. Hold your hands out towards each other at heart level. Your own right hand is placed slightly away from the left hand of your partner, with both right hands facing down, and left hands facing up.

2. Feel a circulation of energy, moving out your right hand, then in through the left hand of your partner and towards their heart. From here it loops up over your partner's head, back to their heart, then out through their right hand and in through your left hand. Then it comes in to your own heart, loops up over your own head, comes back to your heart, and then out again through your right hand. As it loops around the head of both people, it passes through the kunka nawi and qanchis nawi, thus unifying these centers with the sonqo nawi.

3. Allow this circulation to continue by itself, faster and faster. Don't try and visualize or direct the energy too much. Once initiated with your intent, the cellular mind takes over.

4. If you are doing this as a self-treatment, simply bring your hands close to each other at the level of your heart, right hand facing down and left hand facing up, and circulate it through your own body, going from the left hand towards the heart, looping around the head and back to the heart, then out through the right hand and back to the left hand.

CHAPTER 27
THE QANCHIS NAWI

This nawi is the equivalent of the third eye in the yogic tradition. 'Qanchis' means seven, so for the Inka paqo, this is actually the seventh eye. It operates alongside the two physical eyes, lloqe and pana.

In the Gospel of Matthew, Jesus tells his disciples, "The light of the body is the eye. If therefore thine eye be single, thy whole body shall be full of light." He seems to be talking about living a life of integrity expressed in the single-minded pursuit of truth.

Could there be a more esoteric explanation to this as well? Yogic teachings refer to a spiritual eye, capable of seeing God directly. Inka teachings go even further, and speak of unifying this spiritual eye with the two physical eyes, in order to gain a multi-dimensional perspective of life. This way of seeing is known as *qaway*.

In the Kogi tradition, when a child was born with the potential to be a seer, they were raised for some years in the total darkness of a mountain cave, learning how to develop the qanchis nawi. They were able to see the world through the qanchis nawi just as easily as most of us are able to see through our physical eyes. When they were brought back into the village, they served as seers. Their physical eyes were now integrated with their spiritual eye, so they could see multi-dimensionally.

What does it mean for us to see multi-dimensionally, to see through the 'eye that is single'?

Although we may not attain the same level of mastery that the Kogis did, we can begin to learn how to see things as they *are*, rather than as they *appear* to be. In the Advaita tradition, this means learning to identify with the Self rather than with the personal ego.

When the 'I' is single, says Advaita, thy whole body shall be filled with light!

There is a practice of self-enquiry, where you continually refer all your thoughts, feelings and actions to the source where they emanate. It is like a beautiful landscape being reflected on the surface of a lake. The reflection is not real in itself, but mirrors the reality of the landscape around. The clearer the lake the more accurately you can perceive the landscape. But on a windy day with turbulent waves, it is impossible to see the reflection; all you see are turbulent waves.

It is the same with us. There is reflected awareness and there is pure awareness. We are conditioned to believe the personal ego is real in itself, but the one who sees, feels, thinks and acts is actually the Self. When Awareness shines on the mind, you know things, you feel things, you sense things. There is no knowledge independent of that.

The mind is only a lens, the personal ego is only a lens through which the Self experiences the world. To the extent our mind is clear we become pure awareness shining through the personal self, but when the mind is muddy we become identified with the lens itself, with the subtle body, which is limited and temporary.

The mind is a reflected awareness. It is not the knower, even though it may seem so. The ego is not the doer, even though it appears so. You don't need a flashlight to look at the Sun. Likewise, you don't need the mind to know the Self. But you do need the Self to know the mind.

As humans, we experience ourselves as the Self clothed with three bodies But all three bodies, physical, subtle and causal, are perceived objects relative to the Self, like perishable bubbles in a great ocean. Even the soul, our identity within the causal body, is temporary. It does not exist independently from the Self.

Thus, non-duality refers to the knowledge that awareness permeates all things, and this awareness is our deepest essence.

This awareness is deeper than the mind, but that doesn't mean it is difficult to perceive. We just need to quiet the chatter of the mind enough to become aware of this awareness.

The following practice is about separating thought from awareness of thought, becoming aware of who you are as awareness. Don't try and capitalize the Self as if it was something grand and mysterious. It is just the ground of awareness that pervades all things in each ordinary moment. You are simply this awareness, the awareness that is aware of itself within and beyond each thought, feeling, act and emotion experienced by the personal ego.

PRACTICE – AWARENESS OF AWARENESS

Take some time to read the following affirmation of Self, borrowed from a lecture by an outstanding teacher of Advaita, James Swartz. As you read, allow yourself to absorb it fully. Notice the shift in identity as the 'I' becomes single. Notice the deepening sense of Presence. When done with diligence, this mantra is all you will ever need to realize enlightenment.

"What am I? I am limitless, non-dual, pure, awareness. Because I am other than the body, I don't suffer its changes. I am not born, nor do I die. I have no sense organs so I am not involved with the world. Because I am other than the mind, I am free of sorrow, attachment, malice and fear. I am without thought and desire. I have no attributes. I live without breathing. I am eternal, formless and ever free. I am the same in all, and fill all things with being. I am the potential that moves through all things, and manifests as all things. I am limitless, non-dual, pure, awareness."

With practice, you learn to become aware of awareness at all times, which provides a sense of clarity and serenity in the midst of daily life. You will notice that there is a shift in inner identity. You may still use language in the same way as ever, but there will be more depth to your "I" and more space in your "you".

CHAPTER 28
PUTTING IT TOGETHER

Just like the chakras in the yogic tradition, the function of the nawis is to be regulators of sami. As more refined energies flow through, heavier energies are automatically released from the body mind system and into the earth. Simultaneously, as these flows get stronger, the circulation of kundalini gets stronger, your ability to see and hear and feel gets stronger.

You begin to experience more of the upper worlds and lower worlds. You notice that your identity is not as fixed, you become more fluid, more open. You no longer feel as separate from the rest of creation. You begin to realize that who you are in essence is the same awareness that moves through all things. You become a living cell of Gaia.

This awareness of awareness creates a space where you begin to connect with higher levels of the mind. There is more trust in the flow of life. There is more serenity and peace in the midst of outward chaos. You feel empowered to seek your highest destiny. Your eyes open and you begin to see the world in a different way. The outer world may not change so much, but your relationship with it is different.

There is an old story where a king invited all the artists in the city to create a painting depicting the essence of peace. Many beautiful landscapes were created. But the painting that won depicted a world filled with the usual horrors and war. In the midst of all this, however, was a nest high up in the trees, where a bulbul was serenely feeding her chicks.

The following practices, suitable for a small group of people standing in a circle, progressively guide you through all the nawis one by one until they are all open and connected.

PRACTICE – MUNAY MUYU (CIRCLE OF MUNAY)

We will combine saywa taqe with poqpo taqe, standing back to back with one person while working face to face with another. We will then move the energy around the entire circle in a big ring, alternating between these three modes until the energy of the circle merges, enhancing the power of munay. Keep going until one person decides to stop.

1. Make a single big circle, needs to be even number of people. you are paired so that back to back with one partner while face to face with another partner, all the way around.

2. Each person initiates the samin chakuy and saywa chakuy, allowing the electrical and magnetic streams of sami to flow back and forth, opening the doorway between the worlds.

3. Begin the saywa taqe with the person at your back, circulating the energy from the siki nawi, up the back and around with one person, and up the front and around with the other person. Focus on your own half of the circuit, and allow the energy to move faster and faster.

4. Begin the poqpo taqe with the person in front, joining hands at heart level, and circulating the energy out through the right and in through the left, looping around the head in between. Focus on your own half of the circuit, and allow the energy to move faster and faster. You may wish to experiment with a slight distance in between each other's hands.

5. Drop hands and start the circle of munay around the circle, either clockwise or counter-clockwise, faster and faster. Continue until one person says stop.

PRACTICE – HAMPI MUNAY MUYU

Once we learn to generate munay in a circle, we will add one more component, the hampi munay, which involves adding the power of earth and sky to the saywa taqe. As before, make a single circle with an even number of participants, back to back with one partner, and facing another.

1. Back to back – Begin with the saywa taqe, circulating energy around the vertical column, one person in each pairing taking energy up from the siki nawi, with the other bringing energy down to the siki nawi.

2. Front to front - Continue with the poqpo taqe, joining hands, and circulating energy through the horizontal circuit, looping around the head in between.

3. Add the power of the cosmos and the power of mother earth to join these two powers into the circle. The ones who are pulling energy down in saywa taqe will start the samin chakuy, inviting the energy of father cosmos into the munay ring.

4. The ones who are pulling up from siki nawi will start to make saywa chakuy, bringing energy of mother cosmos into the munay ring.

5. Initiate the flow of munay moving around the entire circle in one direction. The energy circulates through the whole wasi (body plus bubble), not just the heart.

6. Choose something we want to heal in ourselves, something we want to change psychologically, physically or spiritually. Take the hucha of this issue and at a given signal put it into the rapidly flowing ring of munay, which transforms and release this heavy energy.

7. Bring munay into your poqpo and body, and finish the exercise.

PRACTICE – DEEP PRESENCE

This practice includes hampi munay muyu but also the qosqo nawi and the physical eyes, incorporating all the nawis one by one. I will take time here to describe each of the steps in more detail for a stronger experience.

1. Stand in a circle, with an even number of people. Turn to face a partner within the circle, with another partner behind you back to back.

2. Start with opening the window at the top of the poqpo. Notice the electric flow of sami moving downwards, followed by the magnetic stream moving upwards. As these streams interact, building in intensity, notice the subtle matrix of light created within each cell of your physical body, extending out through your poqpo. Feel how the presence of others in the circle amplifies the field further. Allow these flows to continue on their own.

3. And now we will do the saywa taqe, activating the vertical column, working with the partner behind you. Bring your attention to the siki nawi, feeling its connection with Mother Earth. All those facing clockwise (an arbitrary choice) in the circle begin to activate the flow of energy going up your own back first, crossing over from crown to crown, coming down your partner's back to the siki nawi, and then returning back full circle. Those facing counter-clockwise are activating the opposite flow, also starting with the siki nawi, but then feeling the flow of energy first going up your partner's back, crossing from crown to crown, and then down your own back. Each person focuses on the half of the energy circuit going through their own body.

4. Let this circulation become stronger and stronger, flowing faster and faster. Do not try and direct the energy with your mind. Once initiated, it moves on its own, under the guidance of the cellular mind. Notice how this vertical circuit joins with the streams already circulating between earth and sky. Feel yourselves extending further and further out as your bubbles join with each other and expand. Allow this flow to continue on its own.

5. Now, focusing on the person in front of you, we will initiate the poqpo taqe, the horizontal circuit, sami moving out the right hand, looping around the head of the other person, coming in through the left hand, circulating around your own head, and then out again through your right hand. Each person focuses on the half of the circuit moving through their own body. Link this

circuit with the vertical channel, and the streams connecting earth and sky. Allow all these flows to continue on their own.

6. Now bring your attention to the qosqo nawi. Each of you now opens the qosqo nawi, focusing primarily on the person in front of you but also on the entire group. We are supporting the entire group in clearing hucha, while the vertical and horizontal flows also continue on their own.

7. So now you have all the nawis open. The window above is wide open, the siki nawi is open through the saywa taqe, the qosqo nawi is open through the hucha mikhuy, and then finally the heart, throat and spiritual eye are open through the poqpo taqe. Allow all these flows to simultaneously continue on their own.

8. And now we are going to send sami clockwise around the entire circle in a ring, whether facing front or back. Feel the munay expanding through the entire wasi to circulate around the circle, joining the other flows.

9. And now we use the two remaining nawis, the physical eyes. Make eye contact with the person in front of you. Allow this to bring you into deeper connection and presence. There is nothing to do, just remain open and connected.

10. Notice all the different manifestations of this energy, joy, laughter, tingling, warmth, vibration. A radiant field of light permeates the entire circle and then far beyond. Sometimes it's a little difficult to contain it all, and each person is free to drop out whenever they wish to. Notice what is happening within the nervous system, within the kundalini channels, your connection with sky and earth, your connection with each other in the circle.

11. Slowly close down the nawis now, and slow down the circulation of sami. Take time to integrate the energies on your own.

PRACTICE – SELF ACTIVATION

The same practice can be done on your own. Find a comfortable place to sit or stand.

1. Open the window of your energy bubble, initiating the samin chakuy and saywa chakuy.

2. Open the siki nawi, and do the saywa taqe, initiating the flow of sami up the back and down the front.

3. Open the qosqo nawi, with the intention to digest whatever hucha is ready to be cleared out at this time.

4. Bring your hands close together at heart level, and open the poqpo taqe or the horizontal channel, circulating energy between heart, throat and spiritual eye.

5. Connect with the Inka muyu, and feel the radiance of this Inner Sun.

CHAPTER 29
THE CHUMPIS

We have moved through the different nawis, learning to distinguish between them and also unify them. Just like the yogic energy system, which includes chakras as well as nadis, the Inka energy system includes nawis as well as *chumpis*, which represent energetic belts and channels.

When Juan Nunez first taught us how to activate the chumpis, he came around to each person, and used a series of *khuyas*, or symbolic stones, to activate corresponding belts and channels. Later, we learned how to do this on our own as an internal practice. It is one of the most powerful practices I know for opening the kundalini energy channels within the body.

There are a few quechua terms that will be important to define before we start the practice. *Pujyu* refers to the fontanelle, a point of energy located on the forehead at the hairline, halfway between between the qanchis nawi and the very top of the head. This is where the spirit, soul and body are united at birth.

The physical body comes from pachamama, birthed at the moment of conception. When we have a body this container attracts the muju, the seed of the Self, a drop of God. The body comes first and then the spirit joins. And then, at the moment of birth we receive the soul. The muju is a spark of divinity that is common to all human beings. What makes us unique is the soul. All the experiences of our lives or even prior lives, our thoughts, feelings, memories and conditioning, are imprinted in the soul.

The point at the very top of the head is known as the *uma*. This represents the joining of spirit with soul, and the beginnings of our individual journey of life. It is where unity consciousness begins to expresses itself in the world of polarity (not necessarily duality).

There are five khuyas used when activating the chumpis with another person, each one symbolically representing a specific numerical property. *Chulla* represents one, *yanantin* represents two, *kinantin* represents three, *tawantin* represents four, and *pisqantin* represents five. The khuyas used by the paqos are ceramic stones, each with a different number of points, to represent these numeric qualities.

Since these khuyas are not easy to find, I created my own medicine bundle, collecting small stones of different colors symbolically representing these same qualities – white for chulla, black for yanantin, red for kinantin, gold for tawatin, and silver for pisqantin.

PRACTICE – CHUMPI AWAY (WEAVING THE BELT) AND NAWI KICHAY (OPENING THE EYES)

1. The first khuya (chulla) activates pujyu (fontanelle). Receiver is standing. The chulla reinforces connection with hanaq pacha as brought down from above and placed on pujya. It can be visualized as the white light of unity consciousness. Take a moment and experience this. The work of the first khuya is now done.

2. You now use the second khuya (yanantin). Starting from pujyu again, pull that energy to uma at top of receiver's head. When it touches uma, the single line differentiates into two lines, running across both sides of the head towards the back of the neck. The white light divides into silver and gold, and travels alongside the two sides of the head down to the back of the neck, the root of kunka nawi

3. Here it changes direction. Turn the khuya 180 degrees, as you prepare to pulling these two cords of gold and silver down the spine and all the way to the siki nawi at the tailbone.

4. The receiver now pulls up a cord of green energy from deep inside mother earth. It is received into the body through the siki nawi and pulled all the way up the spine to connect with the root

of kunka at the back of the neck. The green cord ends at the neck and doesn't go up further.

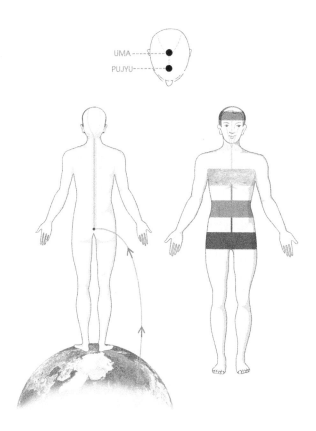

5. So now there are three cords joining at the root of kunka, one that came from the right and goes left (gold), one that came from the left and goes right (silver), and one that comes up from the earth (green). Braid these three cords into one single cord running from top to bottom of the spine. As the three cords merge, it becomes black.

6. Reconnect the yanantin khuya to the siki root, connect with the black energy, and make the first belt at pelvic level, the black belt. Starting with siki nawi at tailbone, you trace a line of energy going under the genitals to the front of the pelvis (being careful not to touch), creating a 'loincloth' that covers the genitals. You then trace the khuya from the front of pelvis towards the rear and returning to the front, first on one side and then the other side. This creates the first of the belts, the black belt.

7. When the black belt is complete, you take the energy up to the second level, qosqo. Replace the yanantin with the kinyantin. Initiate the same movement with the khuyu, although without the loincloth this time, moving front to back, and returning to front, first on one side of the body and then the other. The red belt is built around the body now at this level.

8. When complete, take energy from this belt up to the heart, sonqo. Here replace the kinyantin with the tawantin. Trace the same movements. The red becomes golden, and the golden belt is built around the body now at heart level.

9. When this belt is complete, bring the energy up to the kunka. Now the energy becomes silver. Replace the tawantin with the pisqantin. The silver belt is built around the body now at throat level.

10. Now receiver takes a moment to absorb kausay through all the belts that have been activated.

11. Trace two cords from kunka going up towards the two physical eyes, and then a third cord up to the qanchis nawi, opening the spiritual eye. The work of the khuyus is now done.

12. At this point the receiver receives violet light through the qanchis nawi, filling the body and entire bubble with violet.

When doing this exercise on your own, you don't need the khuyus. Use intention and visualization.

This is a powerful practice for connecting the kundalini flows in your body. When I first learned this practice, I found myself awakening at 4 am every morning for about a month and a half, working the chumpis, opening the nawis, and activating the inka muyu, as we will discuss in the next few chapters. Afterwards, once the circuits became established, an occasional session was enough to maintain the flow.

CHAPTER 30
THE INKA MUYU

You don't have to be in meditation in order to experience oneness. You can be experiencing the awareness of oneness right now, fully present in physical form, in relationship with the world and each other – because there is no other.

Oneness is not just a philosophy of life. It is an integrated state where the three bodies are aware of each other, and find their unity in the Self. It's a state of presence that creates ripples of truth in the world around you. The test of enlightenment is the ability to live in fearlessness and trust, no matter what the circumstances of life. The practices in this book are designed to help achieve this.

The Inka muyu is a reflection of the Sun of Light, present within the human form as a seed of light. As the Inka muyu awakens we discover that there is no separation between this sun and the Sun of Light. That's what enlightenment means from the Inka perspective.

For the paqos, enlightenment is a step-by-step practice of opening the nawis, and then activating the Inka muyu, which means for them becoming the tree of life. If we go back to the Genesis story, there are two trees in the garden. The first is the tree of duality, knowledge of good and evil. As we enter into this world we step into a matrix that has been conditioned by duality. But we do not have to remain there. The next step is returning to unity as the tree of life.

The inka muyu is the seed that grows into the tree, and as it grows into the tree all things are experienced within that tree. All things are connected. I am reminded of *Aywa*, the tree of life in the movie, *Avatar*. The director, James Cameron, had spent some time in the Amazon with the Inka people, working with plant medicines including *Ayahuasca*. Perhaps Ayahuasca became *Aywa*? And perhaps the Navi, the blue people, were inspired by the nawis?

Perhaps *Avatar* represents the world we are stepping into now. As we identify with the Navi, we are identifying with the experience of unity. As the Navi connect with the spirit of Pandora through their braids, they are also linking with each other. When we connect the nawis, we are connecting with the one spirit that moves through all. That's essential what Pandora means.

There is a beautiful series of books by Tom Brown Jr., where he shares the magical world that opens up for him when he encounters an Apache shaman, Stalking Wolf. He often refers to *the spirit that moves through all things*. That's his name for the Great Spirit, God, Brahman, Yahweh, Allah, Aywa. This spirit which moves through all things is the Self, and can be directly experienced as we build the tree of life.

How do we develop a relationship with the Self? In the Indian tradition there are two ways to relate to God. There is the path of self-knowledge where you experience God as your own essential Self, and there is the path of devotion, where you relate to God as a separate entity that could be worshipped with reverence or with passion.

Some people find it awkward to be praying to the Self, but please remember that the same Self is mirrored in all things everywhere. So service to the Self by honoring all creatures you encounter, whether living or non-living, can be the path of ultimate devotion.

Still, for those who find this too vast or too impersonal, the Hawaiian understanding of the high self, middle self and low self may help. The high self, or Aumakua, represents the soul, and is seen as a parental figure, distinct from the Self, that you can communicate with. Multiple gods and goddesses, saints and prophets, across all the spiritual traditions, represent archetypal aspects of the Self, and it is possible to come into personal relationship with them also. For the Sufis, it was simply the Beloved.

The Inka Muyu, this Inner Sun, represents the High Self or the Aumakua or the Beloved. We can learn to develop a relationship with it, just as you can develop a relationship with the earth or cosmos.

PRACTICE – COMMUNICATION THROUGH PRAYER

1. Open the doorway between the worlds. Feel the expansion of presence.

2. Practice the Saywa Taqe and Poqpo taqe, feeling this sense of presence deepen through your energy field.

3. Feel the generation of munay through your body.

4. Let your breath become deep and circular. Conscious breathing generates prana, and the kahunas saw this as the key to communication with the Aumakua.

5. Place your attention on the Inka muyu, located in the solar plexus but also linked with the heart. While maintaining this state of presence, begin a dialogue with this Sun of Light within you, sharing whatever is in your heart to communicate, and then entering a state of deep listening where the High Self can communicate back.

CHAPTER 31
INCARNATING FULLY

The inka muyu can be regarded as a reflection of spirit, or *atman,* as it incarnates within us. It connects us with the soul, a level of identity that extends through many dimensions and many incarnations.

The muju is a spark of divinity that is common to all human beings. What makes us unique is all about the soul. All our experiences of our lives, our thoughts, feelings, conditioning are imprinted in the soul.

The Inkas say that the soul develops through our interaction with the environment, with the apus, and with our ancestral spirits. The Hindus take this further, and assert that the essence of our memories continue after death and get absorbed within the causal body, which represents an eternal soul.

To be fully present with the soul is to recognize that our personal story is part of a greater story of existence, and to honor both as an expression of divine consciousness on this earth.

The following exercises help us incarnate more fully by connecting with our ancestral energy. We will clean our past, including our ancestral past, using the hampi munay.

PRACTICE – WACHAY (ANCESTRAL LINEAGE)

1. Sitting comfortably, create a samin chakuy, bringing cosmic energy down. Experience the lightness of being as sami moves through your wasi, releasing hucha down into the earth.

2. Start recapitulating the events of your life, starting today and going back into the past. If an event carries light energy, make it lighter; if it carries heavy energy, send it into mother earth. Move on to the next memory and continue the same with each event.

3. Go as far as you can go, perhaps even to the moment of conception. If you cannot remember anymore, go to the second step.

4. Bring the energies of your parents to come and share the energy of the samin chakuy, the flow. It doesn't matter if they are dead or alive. If you are adopted, invite all of them. Clean their heavy energies. Once you feel they are adequately light, bring them into your heart and unite them there.

5. Finish the exercise by placing your hands on pachamama. Symbolically adopt her as your mother, and the cosmos as your father. After cleaning all the hucha in your personal story you are giving yourself a new start. Do some saywa chakuy if you like.

Sooner or later we give our bodies back to Pachamama. This moment is called wanuy, the action of dying. What happens to us after this?

The Inka explanation for reincarnation based on the idea that every life is recorded in the earth (akashic record), where it remains. We can have a connection with this trace, flashes and images of these traces. These are not necessarily our own lives, but just as real because we are touching these fields of energy. The entire history of humanity is recorded in the earth. We can connect consciously with these traces, and invite them in so we can grow. We can connect with our roots and our ancestors and be empowered by them.

We receive our bodies and our spirit from the great collective, indistinguishable from anyone else. But it is our soul that makes us unique, that provides us with meaning and identity.

After conception, our first task is to build a body, and to identify with this body. Our task after birth is to build the soul, and to identify with the soul. After we die, the soul returns to the collective, and we reconnect with our identity as spirit. (Note that this is slightly different from the Hindu understanding of the soul, where the subtle body gets reabsorbed into the causal body, including the essential memories of any given incarnation).

The Inka path is about touching life and death through direct experience. Many of our fears are associated with death. The path of power is therefore to consciously pass through death and release these fears, much of which is held within the collective field of human existence.

The following exercise helps to create a bridge between this world and the next, and thus release our fear of death. A big part of our fear of death is the fear of the unknown. When we learn to consciously explore the other side it is no longer quite so frightening!

PRACTICE – WANUY (DYING)

1. Bathe in samin chakuy until you feel the taste of hampi munay (loving healing energy).

2. Imagine you are dying, something specific like a plane crash or a hospital bed or drowning in the ocean.

3. Go through all the details, including all the fear or pain or regrets or attachments. Release these as hucha while you bathe yourself in hampi munay.

4. Cross the boundary, with the intention of touching the energy on the other side

5. Then anchor yourself back in the room with saywa chakuy, while you reaffirm your connection with Pachamama.

CHAPTER 32
PLANTING THE SEED

Each of us is a strand in a living web of life. We are not isolated from the rest of creation. Thus we have many helpers available to us at all times on all levels of existence.

The paqos talk about seven levels of existence. We can receive helpers, or *yanapas*, from each of these levels of existence to prepare us for our own gift of service. First level helpers are cold-blooded creatures, snakes, lizards, crocodiles or dragons, which connect us with the lower world. Second level helpers are animals, who connect us with the middle world. Third level helpers are the winged ones, who connect us with the upper world.

Fourth level helpers are human, perhaps a world teacher who inspires us. Fifth level helpers are masters or avatars. Sixth level helpers are the luminous beings who guide our planetary evolution. Seventh level helpers are galactic beings or divinities.

So the next series of practices is about choosing helpers from each of these seven levels of existence, and establishing a relationship with them by inviting them in one by one into our energy bodies. As we invite the helpers we will simultaneously cleanse the nawis one by one, and plant the seed of life within the earth. Ultimately, this seed will grow into a tree of life, where we experience our connection with the web of living light.

There are several steps to this, which will initially be practiced one by one. Afterwards they can be done together in sequence.

We will take some time to select our team of helpers, and then do a series of seven samin chakuys, each focusing on one of the energy centers.

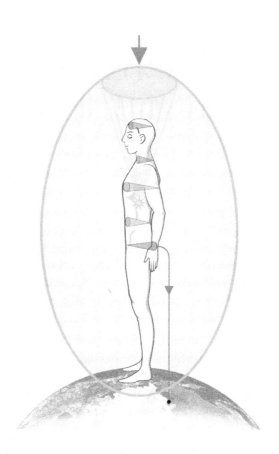

FIRST SAMIN CHAKUY – QAWAY

The first capacity we awaken is Qaway, learning to see. It is not clairvoyant seeing, but the ability to grasp the full potential within something.

Qaway means to use the 3 eyes simultaneously. The qanchis nawi sees the metaphysical aspects of the world, while the two physical eyes ground the vision on planet earth.

Select your team of helpers. Notice which ones you feel most resonance with on each of the different levels, or which ones want to come to you. Fourth level helpers are leaders in their own right, fifth level helpers are incredible healers, and sixth helpers are the wisest people in the world.

1. As you open the bubble, pull the energy down from father cosmos, and let it flow all the way down through the wasi, while giving to mother earth anything that feels heavy.

2. When the energy is flowing all the way through, pay attention to the quality of energy around the three eyes. Sami must be totally refined from top of head to just below the eyes.

3. Make the intention to cleanse heavy energy, starting from the roots of the three eyes. Feel how these 3 cones become totally clean.

4. Absorb sami through the 3 eyes. You will feel a touch in the roots of the 3 eyes where they meet the spine.

5. Then invite the helpers to come down to this area of the 3 eyes (together or one at a time). Pay attention to what their energies feel like. Hold an intention to meet them. We are building a visual connection with our helpers.

SECOND SAMIN CHAKUY – RIMAY.

Here, at this level, we are building rimay, the power to express the truth of our being.

1. Do samin chakuy, release heavy energy all the way down

2. Pull in very refined sami down to just below the kunka nawi, clearing hucha back to front until the entire cone is clean and light.

3. Absorb sami through the clean kunkan nawi and touch the root in the back, next to spine.

4. Invite your helpers into this level, all together or one by one. Allow helpers to express their energies through your voice, one

at a time. Let it be spontaneous. It's not necessarily about how loud the sounds are but noticing how much power these sounds carry.

THIRD SAMIN CHAKUY – KANAY

This time, as we continue doing the samin chakuy, we will bring sami down to touch the inka muyu, located in the solar plexus. This energizes the seed of light, and prepares it for germination in the earth.

1. As sami continues flowing in from the crown, build a funnel, concentrating the sami as it flows towards the inka muyu. Don't worry about precision. It will find the exact point to touch the seed. At this point you will perceive the opening of the seed, like the popping of corn.

2. The essence of the seed will be liberated and melts with the sami coming down. It can then be spread out throughout the body. Some may feel this as a sweet golden nectar. The seed doesn't need to be cleaned since it doesn't have heavy energy. You simply move down the cone and touch the seed with sami.

3. We don't use helpers at this stage, just a concentration of sami touching the seed, and then the seed breaks open, allowing its essence to permeate the whole body.

FOURTH SAMIN CHAKUY – MUNAY

This samin chakuy liberates the quality of compassion within the sonqo nawi, combines it with the power of will as the inka muyu cracks open, and generates munay.

This munay carries our own personal essence. Since there is infinite kausay in the cosmos, we can produce any amount of munay we need in any moment. We become completely independent in terms of munay. We can experience all the love we want for ourselves or to share with another. We can put it into our actions, our words, the food we make, our creative endeavors, and our healing work.

1. Continue the samin chakuy, inviting very refined sami from the cosmos to flow down to just below the sonqo nawi.

2. Cleanse the sonqo nawi back to front.

3. Bring the essence of the seed, the golden nectar that has been liberated, into your heart, joining love and will to generate munay.

4. Invite your helpers into the sonqo nawi now. Feel yourself being embraced together in this space of love.

FIFTH SAMIN CHAKUY –TUSUY

This samin chakuy liberates tusuy, the quality of action, held within the qosqo nawi.

1. Continue bringing energy in from the bubble, and down towards mother earth.

2. Feel refined sami continuing to flow down to just below the qosqo nawi. Focusing on the cone, clean out hucha from back to front. There is generally a lot of hucha here, so spend some time with it.

3. Bring the inka muyu, the seed of light, from its location in the solar plexus, down into the center of the qosqo nawi.

4. Invite the helpers into the qosqo nawi. Allow them to express through movement, one at a time, singing, walking, crawling, dancing as you feel inspired. Remain fully conscious of the seed expressing itself. You are connecting with the source of all life and incorporate it through the whole body as you express it.

SIXTH AND SEVENTH SAMIN CHAKUY – ATIY AND TARPUY

These next two samin chakuys are done together. Atiy is the capacity to accurately measure what you are capable of doing and what you're not. It indicates a quality of fearlessness and self-confidence. Tarpuy represents the planting of the seed into the ground.

1. Continue the samin chakuy, pulling in energy from father cosmos, letting it flow through the wasi, releasing heavy energy into the earth.

2. Bring refined sami to just below the siki nawi, and then start cleaning out the siki nawi. Since the eye of the siki nawi is in the back, we will clean this out front to back. There could be a lot of

hucha at the siki nawi, especially if the qosqo nawi is congested also. Take some time with this, allowing a strong cascade of hucha to flow down from the eye of the siki nawi into the earth.

3. When the siki nawi is absolutely clean, will invite the inka muyu from its current location in the center of the qosqo nawi. Bring it into the root of the siki nawi, and then passing front to back towards the eye.. This exercise is the atiy. It will trigger the capacity to measure your power.

4. Immediately perform the second part of the exercise, tarpuy, sending the seed down from the eye of siki nawi to the earth, planting the inka muyu into the ground.

5. You then invite all the helpers to come and take care of the seed. The seed is planted in pachamama and the helpers will protect this and tend it and help it to become manifested.

6. Allow some time for the inka muyu to feel its connection with Pachamama, and to germinate. Feel it becoming imbued with the qualities of all the helpers and allies.

CHAPTER 33
GROWING THE TREE OF LIFE

We have planted the inka muyu. The seed can now grow into a tree of life, which signifies unity consciousness. As your perceptions change, your priorities change. You become naturally aligned with ayni.

Imagine a mature tree as it becomes a support for other creatures: birds hanging out in the branches, worms crawling among the roots, serpents winding around the trunk. It becomes a haven for many life forms. The Inkas considered themselves guardians of the earth. Being a guardian means enhancing the life of the earth, becoming a steward of the earth.

We imagine we have dominion over the earth, which is basically a justification for rape, slaughter and destruction, which we have done all too well. Being a guardian of the earth is very different. It means protecting, serving, honoring and enhancing the web of life.

Our presence then interacts with the devic kingdoms and angelic kingdoms, changing the flows of life including weather systems and the vitality of ecosystems around. Animals enter your vicinity because they feel welcome, birds start returning, trees grow, butterflies thrive.

It's not survival of the fittest but co-operation between species that drives evolution. Survival of the fittest only has to do with one individual factor. If a herd of deer is being chased by a lion, the weakest gives its body to the circle of life. But it's not about entire ecosystems being destroyed to serve a species that imagines itself superior.

So returning the seed back into the solar plexus represents building a tree of unity. Like Aywa, this tree reflects a delicate web of life where all beings find their safety and strength, their highest expression. As we become this tree of life, our presence becomes a gift to the earth.

For the Inka people this was a given. The ruler of the kingdom was known as the Inka, and Inka means one who is illuminated. Their role was to serve, not to grab, conquer and destroy. As we grow the tree of life we come into the awareness of who we are as guardians and protectors of the earth.

Just as planting the seed is an extension of the samin chakuy, raising the tree is an extension of the saywa chakuy. There are four saywa chakuys in this process.

FIRST SAYWA CHAKUY IS MALLKI CHAKUY

We ask mother earth to send her sami up through our bodies and poqpo, like a tube of light extending up to hanaq pacha. We stand in the middle of this flow.

1. Focus on pulling up a very refined quality of sami up from the earth and through the soles of your feet to just above the level of the siki nawi. This sami moves up the entire wasi, including both body and bubble.

2. Now receive a stream of light coming up from the earth, like a root, directly entering the eye of the siki nawi. Allow this stream to flow from back to front, then flow down between the legs like a loincloth, re-enter the eye of the siki nawi in the back, and then start flowing up the spine.

3. Refined sami continues to rise up through the wasi, flowing up to a level just above the qosqo.

4. When qosqo is covered, receive a stream of light coming directly up from the earth, entering the eye of the qosqo nawi, moving front to back, and meeting the flow of sami coming up

from the siki nawi. These two streams merge and continue rising up the spine.

5. Refined energy continues to rise up through the wasi, flowing up to just about the level of the sonqo.

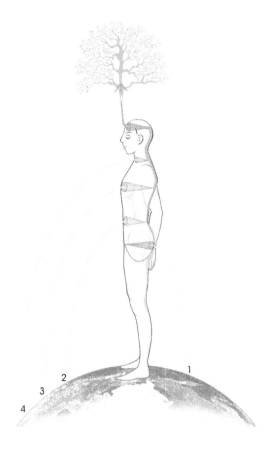

6. When sonqo is covered, receive a stream of light coming directly up from the earth, entering the eye of the sonqo nawi, moving front to back, and joining the two streams already flowing up the spine.

7. Refined sami continues to rise up the wasi to the level just above the kunka.

8. When the kunka is covered, receive a stream of light coming directly up from the earth, entering the eye of the kunka nawi, moving front to back, and joining the three streams already flowing up the spine.

9. Refined sami continues to rise up the wasi through the qanchis nawi and up to the top of the head.

10. The four streams rising up the spine now enter the back of the qanchis nawi. They come out through the three eyes and flow vertically upwards.

11. The column of wasi surrounding you becomes the trunk of the tree of life. The streams coming up through the eyes become the branches and leaves of this tree.

12. Allow the tree to grow as tall and wide as you wish. Notice what kind of tree it wants to become, growing taller and stronger with time.

SECOND SAYWAY CHAKUY IS QANCHIS POQPO.

Qanchis poqpo means seven bubbles. We are expanding the energy bubble to extend out through subtler layers of the aura, all the way out to the causal body. The energy bubble so far has only included the etheric body. Beyond this there are more refined layes of the aura, which we will now link up with. The first part of this exercise is similar to mallki chakuy.

1. Ask pachamama to send her ayni up the soles of your feet and up through the body.

2. Continue the steps for building the trunk of the tree of life, and for receiving the four streams of light up to the back of the qanchis nawi, just like with the mallki chakuy

3. While earth sami continues to flow in from the back of the qanchis nawi towards the front, creating the branches of the tree of life, another stream of the same sami moves up over the top of the head, and then enters the qanchis nawi in the opposite direction. It enters through the three eyes, moves towards the

back of the qanchis nawi, and then continues to move down the spine towards the siki nawi.

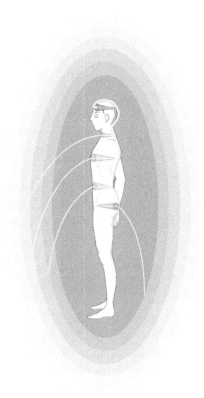

4. So now we have earth sami flowing in both directions up and down the spine, creating a column of highly concentrated, accumulated energy.

5. Focus attention at siki nawi, and feel the entire spine becoming a container for this concentrated energy, like a solid stick of dynamite.

6. Taking a deep breath and expelling it, explode this stick of dynamite. You can use a 'poof', like the merkaba activating breath. The energy explodes out from the entire length of the spine through the body, out through the wasi, and then out in all directions.

7. As a result of this expansion, or explosion, your bubble will differentiate into seven layers, like an onion of seven layers extending for enormous distances all around you.

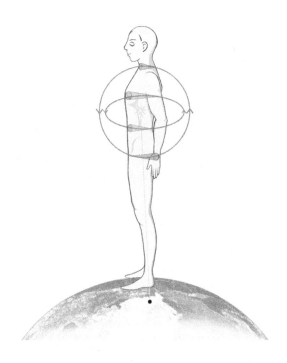

THIRD SAYWA CHAKUY IS TAWANTIN

This next step is about bringing back the inka muyu to its home in the solar plexus, and then linking it energetically to the different nawis. We will be weaving together the four qualities associated with these four nawis: atiy, or impulse in the siki nawi, khuyay, or passion in the qosqo nawi, munay, or compassion in the sonqo nawi, and rimay, or integrity in the kunka nawi. We thus make a despacho, or offering, to send out to the world.

1. It is now time to take the seed back up from the ground. We will use the axis that goes through the center, the sushumna. We pick it up from the earth, through the perineum and back inside the kunay (solar plexus area) where it originated. But there will remain a cord that always connects the seed with the earth.

2. Feeling the power of the earth joining with the inka muyu, we now connect the inka muyu with the qosqo nawi below and the sonqo nawi above, spinning the energy of the inka muyu around these two centers, faster and faster, until these centers are woven together.

3. Pull up more power from the earth into the inka muyu, and now connect the seed with the siki nawi below and the kunka nawi above. Once again spin the energy around these two centers, faster and faster until the centers are woven together.

4. The functions of these nawis are now linked together. We can also send this woven energy out as a despacho, a sacred gift to hanaq pacha or ukhu pacha or any of the apus, (guardian spirits of the earth) either with a request or with thanksgiving.

FOURTH SAYWA CHAKUY IS AMARU

The final step in the tree of life is to experience the amaru, or anaconda, rising up from the earth and becoming the protector for the tree of life. In the Genesis story the serpent is represented as a tempter, responsible for our fall into duality. Now, the same serpent becomes a protector, guarding the tree of life so we can experience our natural unity with all things.

1. Make a saywa chakuy with mother earth, pulling up a column of light around your wasi, and sending it up through the top of your head. This is the trunk of the tree of life.

2. Bring the four streams of light, as earlier, flowing up from the earth to the siki nawi, (making a loop around the genitals), then the qosqo nawi, then the sonqo nawi and then the kunka nawi. These streams join together up the spine and move up.

3. From the back of the qanchis nawi, these combined streams move towards the front, exit through the three eyes and up into the sky, as you continue building the tree of life. This part of the exercise is exactly the same as mallku chakuy earlier.

4. Now focus on an area behind you. Open a hole there at ground level.

5. Invite your amaru, or anaconda protector, to come up from this hole. Feel her coming up behind you, touch the back of siki nawi, then move all the way up the spine till she is

overshadowing you. She is not inside your body, but rather entwined up the spine. Most of her body is still within the earth, connecting with the powerful energies of Pachamama.

6. Pay attention to the color. Usually she comes out green. Visualize her becoming black to match the first belt, built around the sacrum.

7. Then visualize her becoming red to match the second belt, built around the belly.

8. Then visualize her becoming silver to match the fourth belt, built around the throat.

9. Then visualize her becoming gold, the color of the third belt, built around the heart.

10. The energy of mother earth is infinite, and you can ask for all the energy you need. If you need to experience a sense of safety or security in your life, the anaconda will be black. If you need to transmute hucha, she will become red. If you need to communicate or explore your creative energy she will become silver. If you simply wish to remain in your heart, she will become gold.

This concludes the practice of planting the seed and building the tree of life. The extended samin chakuy helps to clear vast amounts of hucha from your wasi, and the extended saywa chakuy helps you receive the deep healing power of the earth. Continue building your relationship with the helpers. As their energy, light and wisdom become anchored within your wasi, you will be able to draw power and inspiration from them whenever needed.

Although these practices for activating the inka muyu may seem long at first, you can learn to do them very quickly. You may wish to work on these two sequences every day for some time until the tree feels firmly anchored within your being.

CHAPTER 34
FINDING YOUR CENTER

The practices in the next few chapters come from the Kayawaya tradition of Bolivia, which is closely allied with the Q'ero traditions of Peru. They were received by Don Juan Nunez del Prado from Tata Lorenzo in La Paz.

Once we have we have learned to work with the basic aspects of energy transmutation, such as samin chakuy, saywa chakuy, hucha mikhuy, chumpis and inka muyu, we can move on to establish our links with the infinite universe.

Each of us has seven cords through which we make our connections with the universe. A cord is known as *seqe*, hence these connections are known as the *qanchis seqe*.

These connections are empowering us all the time, whether we are conscious of them or not. They operate through space, through time, and through the social realms. We can learn to empower ourselves consciously.

The first two connections link us up to the worlds of space, the next two connections link us up with our families, and the last two connections link us up with the world of time.

The first seqe goes up to the hanaq pacha, the upper worlds. You connect here with Wiracocha, or the Cosmic Father.

The second seqe goes down to the ukhu pacha, the lower worlds. You connect here with Pachamama, or the Cosmic Mother.

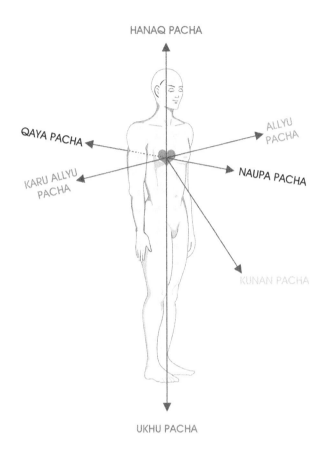

HANAQ PACHA

QAYA PACHA

ALLYU PACHA

KARU ALLYU PACHA

NAUPA PACHA

KUNAN PACHA

UKHU PACHA

The third seqe, going out towards the left, is our *allyu*, our close family. This is not necessarily just blood family, but represents the people in our lives that support us on a soul level. There could typically be about 30 people in the world who are our true family. We send out a seqe to connect with our support group.

The fourth seqe, going out towards the right, is our *karu allyu*, our distant family, ideally representing all of humanity. We send out a seqe to connect with our entire human family.

Directly in front of us is the *naupa pacha,* the fifth seqe, which represents the past. We go back and connect to the moment of our conception.

Directly behind us is the *qaya pacha,* the sixth seqe, which represents the future. We go forward and connect with the moment of our death.

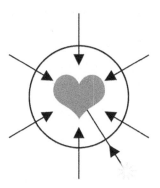

Then finally, in the center, we find the seventh seqe, the *kunan pacha,* which represents the present moment. Here in the center we find the inka muyu, and make a connection with the seed of light.

Being a healer requires the ability to generate munay. Making a cord linking the seed with your heart is another way to create munay. In order to feel love for a person, you must be in the body, and present in this moment. This is the path with heart that Castaneda talked about.

PRACTICE – QANCHIS SEQE AND QANCHIS SAMIN CHAKUY

1. This exercise is done on your own.

2. The first step, the qanchis seqe, is to create the cords using your intention. As you make the intention within the bubble, send six cords out to hanaq pacha and ukhu pacha, then to ayllu pacha and karu ayllu pacha, and finally to naupa pacha and qaya pacha.

3. Then we make the seventh connection. Pull a cord from your seed, located in the solar plexus, to connect with your heart.

4. The second step is to empower all these connections. The cord from the seed is already in your heart. Bring the other six connections from the bubble into the heart also. You are pulling energy from all your sources of support to empower the heart. This step is known as the qanchis samin chakuy.

5. Feel your place in the universe now. You are bringing yourself into the present, which is your place of power. The present moment is the only place where you can experience and express your power.

6. As you do this exercise you may notice that some of the cords are not as strong as the others, so you can improve these through your ayni. You can consciously pull power from the source anytime you want.

CHAPTER 35
SEEDS OF LIGHT

The inka muyu is the seed of light, a reflection of the Great Spirit as it connects with our individual human structure. It is located within the solar plexus. It is the center of our will.

In an earlier exercise we planted this seed into the ground in order to build the tree of life. In this exercise we will now bring the seed into each of the nawis in turn, planting them there for a moment, and illuminating them with its highest quality of unified light.

We will include not only the nawis within the body but also a center above the head and a center below the feet. These centers are still within the bubble, but since the hanaq pacha begins just above the top of the head, and the ukhu pacha begins just below the bottoms of the feet, these points are known as the *personal hanaq pacha* and the *personal ukhu pacha*.

As you move the inka muyu you are building a tube of light that runs all the way between the ukhu pacha and hanaq pacha, and as wide as the poqpo itself.

Afterwards we will create a channel of concentrated light between these two points, including all the nawis in between. We will then send it out through the four directions across the universe.

PRACTICE – QINSE PACHA SEQE

1. Invite your helpers into your bubble.

2. Bring your attention to the inka muyu, located just below the sternum in the solar plexus.

3. Bring this seed up to the sonqo, planting it in the center of the sonqo nawi for a moment until you experience its light illuminating the entire heart.

4. Bring this seed up to the kunka, planting it in the center of the kunka nawi for a moment until you experience its light illuminating the entire throat.

5. Bring this seed up into the three eyes, planting it in the center of this region until you experience its light illuminating all the eyes.

6. Bring this seed up to the personal hanaq pacha, planting it here for a moment, until you experience its light shining brightly.

7. Now returning the seed to its original location, start moving it downwards into the qosqo, planting it in the center of the qosqo nawi for a moment until you experience its light illuminating the entire belly.

8. Bring this seed into the siki, planting it the center of the siki nawi until you experience its light illuminating the entire pelvis.

9. Continue to bring this seed down into the personal ukhu pacha, planting it here for a moment until you experience its light shining brightly.

10. Notice that there is an axis extending all the way from the hanaq pacha to the ukhu pacha. You will now concentrate the power of this axis, building a channel of light known as the qinsa pacha seqe.

11. Make a samin chakuy. Opening the bubble wide, bring down the energy of the cosmos from Wiracocha. Let it become concentrated as it moves down this channel, and through the places we have planted the seed.

12. Make a saywa chakuy, asking Pachamama to send sami up the channel, concentrating it to fill the channel all the way to the top, making it stronger and stronger until there is solid contact

all the way from ukhu to hanaq pacha. It is now perhaps a few centimeters in diameter.

13. Feel within the siki nawi to know when you have enough energy available for the next step, which is to make ayni with all the forces of the universe.

14. When there is enough energy in the channel, send energy we have concentrated in the seqe out horizontally in the four directions, honoring your close family, your distant family, your moment of conception, and your moment of death. Touch them all simultaneously.

15. This time it is not an explosion, as with creating the qanchis poqpo, but a strong continuous flow in all four directions.

CHAPTER 36
SHARING HEALING GIFTS

Much of what we have learned so far is to prepare your own wasi and subtle bodies for deeper awareness. Now we will use the healing energy we have accumulated to work with clients.

The first thing to do is to attune with the hampi munay, the healing energy that arises from the blending of heart and will. This is the key. It is the energy that heals, not the techniques or the feathers or other sacred objects. Touch is important, to the extent possible, along with the intention for healing. The following practice is known as *Pichay*, which means sweeping.

In the North American tradition, this is usually done using an eagle feather for clearing heavy energy. In Central and South American traditions, this is often done with the use of a medicine bundle, or *micha*, which is a collection of sacred stones and other charged objects.

This is a samin chakuy, meaning that we move energy in a descending flow of light, clearing hucha accumulated within the body down to the earth. The practitioner focuses their breath as they touch different parts of the body with the micha.

PRACTICE – PICHAY MIKHUY

1. Prepare yourself with samin chakuy, saywa chakuy and hucha mikhuy if needed.

2. Use micha to sweep out hucha through each of the nawis, siki, qosqo, sonqo, kunka, pana, lloqe, and qanchis.

3. Use micha to sweep out hucha through each of the rhapys, siki, qosqo, sonqo, kunka, pana, lloqe, and qanchis.

4. Use micha to clear the kurku, or spine.

5. Use micha to clear the uma (crown), maki (hands) and chaki (feet).

6. Use micha to clear the pujyu (fontanelle), where the body, soul and spirit come together at birth and separate at death.

7. Use micha to touch face, back, neck, shoulders, chest, back, arms, legs.

8. Develop a routine, doing same routine each time so you don't miss anything.

PRACTICE – HOQARI KALLPACHI

The complement to Pichay is called hoqari kallpachi. Hoqari means to rise, kallpachi means to give power, to empower.

If Pichay is a samin chakuy, working with downward energy, Hoqari Kallpachi is a saywa chakuy, working with upward healing energy.

Whereas the pichay is for clearing hucha, the hoqari kallpachi is to empower a person who is feeling weak.

1. Take the micha and make the intention to take the power of mother earth up, covering the person with the power of mother earth. It is for a person who is feeling weak.

2. Go through exactly the same routine, but this time with raising energy at each of the points.

CHAPTER 37
LINKING UP TO THE COSMOS

I will share one last practice from the Inka tradition. Although based on the same cosmovision, this one was created directly by Don Juan Nunez del Prado, and his son Don Ivan Nunez del Prado, so is offered here as a tribute to their untiring mission of bringing this ancient tradition forward in this time of pachakuti.

Rather than white light, we will use the power of the black light this time, the same black light that we created when making the chumpis, or belts. This black light is the light of creation, and is known as *willka*. We will also be experiencing the power of the belts. Each belt has its own color, and we will be synchronizing these colors with the powers of the cosmos.

For those who may be wondering, our use of black light has nothing to do with any form of black magic. The Inka cosmovision doesn't operate within the realm of duality. The black light is the power of creation that comes from the earth. It is the darkness within which the seed germinates and gives form to endless life.

Tarpuy means planting. We will be planting the seed deep within the heart of the Earth, then inside the heart of the Sun, a guiding Star, and finally the center of the Galaxy. We will take with us the power of the black light as the seed travels out to these realms, returning back with specific gifts of energy from each of these realms.

PRACTICE – COSMIC TARPUY

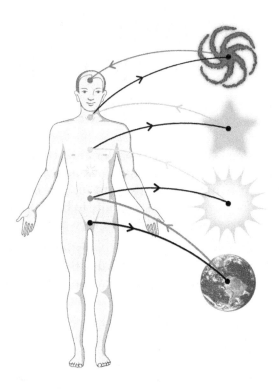

1. Take the seed from within its home in the solar plexus, and bring it into the siki nawi. Bathe it in the power of willka generated within the spine and within the black belt until the inka muyu also becomes black.

2. Send your seed into the earth, but this time deep into the center of the earth. Within the earth, under the magma, there is the concentrated power of black iron magnetite. Send your seed all the way down to this center.

3. Plant your seed here, then bring it back and plant it in the qosqo nawi. As it passes through the magma it will pick up the red energy of the magma. Bring this energy into the qosqo nawi, permeating it with red light.

4. Then the seed becomes black again. Now send it from the qosqo nawi towards the Sun. Plant it in the dark center of the Sun, a black hole in the middle of the sun that connects it with all things.

5. Plant the seed here, then bring it back and plant it in the sonqo nawi. As it returns, it collects golden energy from the Sun's corona, permeating the heart with the golden energy of the Sun.

6. Then the seed becomes black again. Now send it from the sonqo nawi out to your guiding Star. It could be any star that you feel a special connection with, perhaps Sirius or Arcturus or Polaris. Each time you connect with your Star the cord becomes stronger. The paqos say that when you die, your guiding star becomes your pointer, showing you which way to go.

7. So send the seed to your star, plant it there for a moment, and then bring it back to the kunka nawi. As it returns, it brings back the radiant silver energy of the Star, permeating the kunka nawi with it.

8. The seed becomes black again. You then send your seed out to the center of the galaxy, which has seven rings surrounding it and six spiral arms extending out into space. You plant your seed into the dark womb of the galactic center.

9. Our galaxy has a violet hue to it. As you seed returns, it carries this violet energy back with it. Plant it in the qanchis nawi.

10. Now visualize the entire galaxy in front of you with its dark womb of creation, the 6 arms, and the violet hue. This image creates a paradigm shift, just like when astronauts first saw the earth from outer space. It expands your capacity to create higher realities.

11. As shared in an earlier chapter, astrophysicist Paul LaViolette, refers to the center of the galaxy as a Mother Star. It generates a tremendous creative power, which travels out on galactic pulses every twelve thousand years to activate a new world age. As we complete this exercise, we are bringing back this creative power inside our seed, to prepare us for the taripay pacha, the age of light to come.

12. Let the inka muyu remain in the qanchis nawi for a while, infusing it with galactic consciousness, before returning it to its place within the solar plexus.

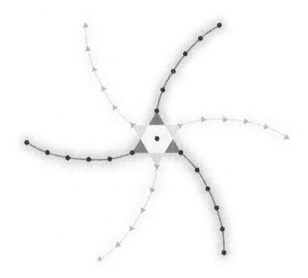

PRACTICE – DANCING THE GALAXY AWAKE

This is a choreographed meditation, performed with a group of people to mirror the movements of our galaxy. Our galaxy has six arms, according to the paqos, and so this meditation is known as Soqtantin, or six.

1. First we will create the center. Invite three men and three women into the center, creating one circle alternating men and women. Men reach out to hold hands with the other men, while women reach out to hold hands with the other women in a basket weave. Each person receives energy from the person on

the left, makes an energy loop around the head, then sends out to the person on the right.

2. The rest of the group lines up behind these six people in the center, men behind men and women behind women, placing hands on the shoulders of the person in front of them. This configuration represents the spiral arms of our galaxy.

3. The six people in the center peform a saywa chakuy with the earth. The rest of the people receive this sami, allow it to flow through, and experience the galactic energy as it spirals through them. The last person in line sends the sami back to the earth, creating a loop with Pachamama.

4. The six people in the center begin to rotate clockwise, with the rest of the people following accordingly. Walk faster and faster to represent the galactic flows.

5. Stop. Feel within you the movement of galactic sami, which is also the ilahinoor field, or the supramental light. Let it permeate all the cells of your body. You are building a galaxy inside you. Visualize our solar system within one of the galactic arms, held within a vast network of electrical filaments. Remain for a moment, joining heaven and earth, and then finish the exercise.

The seed is a point where you can receive your Self. Your spiritual being and your psychological being come together here.

Once you have planted your seed in the center of the galaxy you can do anything. The earth has become your home, the solar system has become your home, the galaxy has become your home.

The seed can also take you into the past or the future. You can do anything you want with your seed, but keep it inside you. Always bring it back.

You have created a map of the universe now, which includes not only the kai pacha but also the hanaq pacha and the ukhu pacha. You also have your compass, the inka muyu and the helpers, to guide you onwards.

I would like to end this section with two further practices from the Eastern traditions.

CHAPTER 38
THE SOUND CURRENT

The following practice comes from the Himalayan traditions, which I find very complementary to the Inka, Ilahinoor and Advaita traditions. The *sound current*, or divine sound, is a foundational practice for linking directly with the soul, or aumakua, and is common to many Hindu, Sikh, and Sufi meditation practices.

When electricity runs through a power line it produces a humming sound. Likewise, when higher spiritual energies run through the circuitry of the human body, there is an interface between the two energy fields that we can hear within our heads as a current of sound. All creation is a manifestation of sound, the eternal OM. This same sound can be heard and felt within our own bodies. You might first experience this as a very subtle, almost subliminal, tone. Later, or in deeper states of meditation, it can become so loud it drowns out everything else through its vibrancy.

Experience of the sound current varies depending on the degree of one's inner attunement. You might hear it as a buzzing or a ringing, or as the sound of waves along the shore. It could be a clear ringing tone or the roar of thunder. However it is first experienced, as you bring your attention to that sound it becomes stronger and more coherent until it eventually merges into the music of the spheres.

The sound current is a very sweet sensation of subtle sound. In the beginning it might help to cover the ears or go someplace absolutely quiet. As you become more accomplished with this practice, you hear this tone constantly, and it serves as a continuous link with the soul. You might notice that this pitch changes as your brain wave rhythms change. It also changes when you are in the presence of higher vibrational beings.

You can begin to distinguish the energies of various interdimensional beings by the difference in tone. Likewise, when you are out in nature, taking the time to soak in the vibrancy of sounds and colors, you begin to notice changes in the sound current as you connect with various elemental energies and nature spirits. As you match frequency with another being through the sound current, you might experience deeper levels of communication.

This same principle applies to areas within your own body. The state of cellular health matches the frequency to which it vibrates. As we pay attention to the sound current, it lifts the vibrational frequency of each cell into greater octaves of health and vibrancy. You begin to communicate with your cells and they begin to communicate with you. Eventually this transforms the cellular frequency, freeing up emotions and physical disease.

Most people first experience this tone inside the head sometimes closer to one ear or the other. In Shabda Yoga the sound current is said to usually enter through the right ear. Notice where you hear this sound current. Over time you may find that you begin to hear it through every cell of your body.

You begin to observe how it corresponds with various sensations. Eventually the denser tones and frequencies give way to subtle currents of blissful light.

PRACTICE – SOUND CURRENT

1. Find a quiet place where you can simply listen. Allow yourself to become aware of distinct sounds around you. As you deepen into this receptive mode, begin to notice the sound current - a sound emanating inside your own head. It may sound like crickets buzzing or a bell tolling, like waves on the seashore, or a

high-pitched hum. Notice what you hear and simply deepen into it.

2. As you attune you may become aware of more than one frequency of sound. Simply focus on the highest tone you become aware of.

3. Notice where you experience this tone. In some traditions it is recommended to focus on the tone closer to the right ear, while in other traditions it is preferable to focus close to the center of the head. Eventually it will become a resonance that pulses through the entire head and even through every cell of your body.

4. If you cannot hear the sound current at first, simply cover your ears with the palms of your hands. Notice what you hear. Begin with that. See if you can maintain this link with the sound current — this link with the frequencies of your soul — for as long as possible.

CHAPTER 39
VIPASSANA MEDITATION

The practice of Vipassana is an ancient Buddhist teaching for experiencing full body enlightenment through the awareness of sensations. In recent years it has been revived in India by the Burmese teacher, Goenkaji, and is typically taught by associate teachers around the world as a 10 day intensive.

The term *vipassana* means insight – insight into the truths of impermanence, suffering, and liberation from suffering. The Buddha taught that sensations in the body are the doorway to the deepest levels of the mind, and therefore the deepest levels of enlightenment.

Energy follows attention and as we bring our awareness into our body, its vibrational resonance begins to change. We find over time that what we have experienced as gross matter is teeming with subatomic currents of light. As we enter into these currents, we experience ourselves in bodies of light. This is a prelude to the experience of true matter that Sri Aurobindo and the Mother referred to.

We begin by learning to simply experience things for what they are, without trying to change anything, without trying to repress unpleasant sensations, without craving for pleasant sensations. As we experience sensations for what they are, we experience the loosening of *vasanas*, or karmic knots, in the subconscious mind.

We begin with an awareness of breath as it passes in and out of the nostrils, and then the sensations experienced with this subtle flow of breath. This helps to concentrate the mind for the next part of the practice.

We then bring our attention back and forth through the body, starting with the top of the head and going down to the feet, then from the feet back up to the head, all the while remaining in a state of equanimity. Like the sound current, the practice of vipassana meditation is deceptively simple yet capable of leading us to the highest realms of spiritual experience.

Emotions may come up to be cleared. As that happens, we simply look to see where we experience those emotions and translate them into sensations in the body. It is not important to process these through the mind. When observed without resistance and without attachment, they simply dissolve. Profound physical and emotional healing is possible in this manner, as are deep levels of Self-realization.

The following practice combines the sound current and vipassana meditation.

PRACTICE – VIPASSANA MEDITATION

1. Listen to the sounds around you, reaching out with all of your senses as you listen. Listen for each sound, the spaces between the sounds, letting the external sounds take you deeper and deeper into the silence within. Turn your attention inwards. Listen to the sound current in the center of your head as you let your breath become slow and subtle. It can be either subliminal or audible.

2. Become aware of your breath as it enters the nostrils and as it moves out. Become aware of the sensations here. Remain with this awareness until your mind becomes concentrated.

3. Now, bring your attention to the top of your head, and become aware of whatever sensations you experience there — it could be vibration, pulsing, tingling, throbbing, pressure, or pain. There could be heat, coolness, or subtle electrical energies. You may experience numbness or the absence of any feeling. It is not necessary to find a name for what you are experiencing; just

experience whatever it is that you are sensing without trying to change anything.

4. Slowly move your attention through different parts of your body. From the top of your head, bring your attention into your forehead and along the temples, along every part of the scalp, and then the eyes, and deep into the eyeballs. Become aware of sensations, and simultaneously listen beyond the sensations to the sound current.

5. Gradually move down to your nose, your cheeks, out to your ears, down to your mouth, your lips, chin, and jaw. Move down the back of the neck, down to the throat, side to side and front to back.

6. As you bring your attention to every part of your body, surface as well as deep, it begins to wake up. Make sure you are experiencing actual physical sensations directly within the body, rather than something only visualized in your mind's eye.

7. Move from the throat down any one shoulder to the elbow, hand, tips of the fingers. Become aware of any tightness, any soreness, any tingling or vibration or pulsing, the grosser sensations as well as the subtler sensations, surface as well as deep. Then go down the other arm.

8. Keep your breath circular. Become aware of places where you tend to hold your breath. This is where energy patterns have become stuck in the body.

9. Move your attention down the front of your body - from the throat down to the chest, the lung cavity, the rib cage and the sternum, down through your heart and the internal organs. Slowly move down to the abdominal area, the solar plexus, the belly, the internal organs in your belly cavity, down to the pelvis and the genitals. Continue being aware of sensations.

10. Move down the back, starting with the shoulders and the shoulder blades, experiencing sensations within your spine, the muscles along your back, the tissues, and the bones. Slowly move down to the middle back and then the lower back and buttocks.

11. Allow your awareness to penetrate right through the body, from the front of the body through the center and out the back,

and then returning to the front. Let your breath become subtle. The more subtle the breath, the more you can feel the subtle sensations.

12. From the buttocks, move your attention down one leg, from the thigh, down to the knee and the lower leg, down to the ankle, foot and toes. Continue with the other leg.

13. Switch directions, returning back up to the head. After a couple times of going back and forth, you can start moving simultaneously through the arms and legs.

14. Once you become aware of your body part by part, you can also sweep rapidly through the body, experiencing a flow of energy through the electrical channels. Alternate between the two modes.

15. Get a sense of your body as a single unit. Become aware of the sound current. See if this has changed or deepened, and listen again to all the sounds within and without, noticing how you've become a part of each sound. A subtle current of sound vibrates through your entire body, taking you into a deep stillness. Remain in this stillness for as long as you wish.

PART III

THE DESTINATION

Homo Luminous

Was there ever a longing
Without its fulfillment?
Is the bee ever drawn
To a nectarless flower?
Then why bang my head on walls?
I have identified with doing
When all I am
Is a vessel waiting to be emptied
I am so full of myself
Ideas, expectations, even the longings
What remains if I surrender it all?
True surrender is an act of grace
In letting go I am already filled
In giving up control
Every dream I have ever had
Finds its home
Simple yet not easy
It takes a million years to realize
That it only takes an instant
I've hit bottom in a bottomless pit of illusion
I am ready for you now beloved Friend!

Kiara Windrider

CHAPTER 40
LEVELS OF AWARENESS

From the perspective of the Self there is only one consciousness that permeates all things, and which expresses through all things. This consciousness includes all memories of the past, all potentials for the future, all physical manifestations, all forms of intelligence in all realms and dimensions of life. There is no greater or lesser, no levels or distinctions.

From the perspective of human consciousness, we can be more or less clouded in our understanding of this, and hence there is a hierarchy of levels which marks our journey of remembrance.

The Inkas talk about seven levels of awareness. It represents our journey from unconsciousness into the full light of Consciousness. Those of us on the first level are relatively unconscious of anything beyond the illusion of separation. We live exclusively in the middle world, ignorant of spiritual realities and disconnected from the intelligence of nature.

On the second level we are becoming aware of morality and ethics as a means of relating to the world. We realize that we are not an island, and have responsibilities to each other and to the world. We cannot destroy the earth or hurt somebody else without suffering the consequences.

On the third level we begin to live in accordance with the golden rule. We learn about ayni, the law of reciprocity. We learn that rather than keeping a tally of how much we receive in exchange for what we give, the highest form of ayni is unconditional giving. In contrast to Hindu philosophy, which believes in a karmic balance that gets carried from lifetime to lifetime, the Inka paqos say that we start and end every life with a clean slate, and the only measure of what we leave behind is the quality of our ayni.

On the fourth level we learn to broaden our perspectives. The doorway between the worlds is wide open, and we are able to move past nationalistic or religious dogmas to embrace the universal essence of all things. We have perfected the laws of ayni, and experience a beautiful dance of synchronicity where we find ourselves always in the right place at the right time with the right people for what needs to be accomplished through us.

A key ingredient at this level is the ability to synthesize. Leonardo da Vinci, the quintessential Renaissance Man, was a prime example of this. He was a painter, a philosopher, a mathematician, an inventor, an educator, and a mystic. At this level you begin to transcend the limits of your conditioned mind, and enter the higher levels of the mind.

The fifth level is about becoming a creator. There are not many fifth level initiates in the world today. The Inkas say that a fifth level paqo, or Mallku Inka, would be capable of healing all physical conditions. They have integrated the functions of munay, yachay and llankay to a point where they can become a clear channel for luminous beings to step through.

At the sixth level you become luminous yourself. There is an Inka prophecy that at the turning of the ages six men and six women will rise up, fifth level initiates capable of healing anything. Through the field they create together will emerge the Sapa Inka, a luminous couple immersed in the Sixth level of awareness, who will lead the world into the Taripay Pacha, where humanity can once again see its true face.

The seventh level is the Spirit that moves through all things. We can call this what we wish, until we learn to see this as our own true Self, at which point no names become necessary.

As with parallel systems from Egyptian, Theosophical and Buddhist traditions, these levels of initiation are not certificates of merit to be hung up on a wall. They are written in your heart, and represent a commitment to serve humanity in the best way you can, giving freely with no expectation of return.

There is a teaching story that may be relevant to understanding these levels in daily life. It is the story of each of us on our journey, an Autobiography in Five Chapters.

In chapter 1, I am walking down the road. There is a big hole in the middle of the road. I don't see it, and I fall in. I immediately begin to blame everybody else for why I fell down the hole, meanwhile digging myself in even deeper.

In chapter 2, I am walking down the same road. There is the same hole in the middle of the road. Again, I don't see it, and fall in. This time time, rather than blame, self-pity and guilt take over, and I start whipping myself for all the miserable choices I've ever made in my life. I am still digging myself deeper into the hole.

In chapter 3, I am still walking down the same road. I see the hole in front of me, but conditioned by habit, fall in anyway. I am no longer trapped in guilt, shame or blame, however, and quickly find my way back out.

In chapter 4, I am still walking down the same road, which again has a big hole in the middle of it. I choose to avoid falling in, and walk around it.

In chapter 5, I take a different road!

As long as I am trapped in the illusion of separation, I keep falling into the traps of guilt, shame, limitation and blame. But once I come out of the illusion, I recognize that the universe is a friendly place, and enter into relationship with it. By the time I get to chapter 5, I have become a creator, recognizing that I no longer need to learn through suffering, and that I have come to make the world a better place. The universe supports me on a path of ayni, characterized by beauty, grace, abundance and freedom.

This is the path with a heart.

CHAPTER 41
KUNDALINI AWAKENING

As we proceed along the initiatory path, our perspectives change. As we start entering a deeper flow of life, layers of hucha that have been locked deep into our subconscious mind, begin to release. This opens up a greater flow of life energy in the body, which in the yogic tradition is known as *kundalini*.

Doorways between the worlds open wider, and the mind starts becoming more permeable. We are no longer stuck in a purely rational perspective but can begin to open to the more expanded levels of the mind, which Sri Aurobindo refered to as the higher mind, the illumined mind, the intuitive mind, the overmind, and finally the Supermind.

The spiritual path is often marked by periods of expansion followed by phases of contraction. Each time we release a layer of hucha, more light comes in which must be absorbed and integrated. As it integrates, further layers of hucha are released, and the process continues.

As hucha is released from the nervous system and from the energy centers, it opens these channels to a greater flow of light. This can be a joyful and exhilarating process. However, the release of hucha can also trigger traumas and memories that have been buried deep in the subconscious, which rise into consciousness on their way out.

We have a choice here. If we are able to simply witness these old patterns without going into a spiral of guilt, shame or judgment, they quickly pass, and more sami comes through. It is also important to have a strong connection with earth and sky, so that sami from the upper worlds can continue to release accumulations of hucha into the earth, and the earth can support a next phase of healing and integration.

However, there are times when there is too much conscious or subconscious resistance, which creates a healing crisis within the body, generating symptoms of kundalini overload.

There is a term, *spiritual emergency,* sometimes used to describe a kundalini overload, which could include a full range of symptoms from intense heat to inflammation in the joints to heart palpitations to involuntary twitching to extreme sensitivity of body and senses. There can be difficulty sleeping or relaxing. The mind feels overwhelmed, and dysfunctional emotional patterns are easily triggered. We begin to forget names, faces and non-essential details.

However, if we remain grounded and neutral, embracing these symptoms as part of a deeper integration of light, they quickly pass. We begin to experience an opening of the subtle senses. We connect with higher levels of the mind. We develop a spontaneous relationship with the elemental forces around. We begin to experience states of spontaneous bliss, and the heart opens to a boundless ocean of love. Subtle electrical currents flood through the body.

Sometimes there is a tendency to get overly attached to these blissful symptoms, in which case the attachment itself creates stagnation within the energy field, followed by a collapse or depression. But the channels, once opened, cannot close down so easily, and sooner or later there is another episode of ecstasy or bliss. People sometimes fluctuate back and forth between these states for a long time before eventually stabilizing at a higher level.

Most of us are so mired in duality that we tend to interpret ecstatic experiences as being more spiritual, or even somehow a sign that we have become enlightened. And so when the time comes that we inevitably return to more ordinary states of consciousness, we feel that we have done something wrong, or lost our enlightenment.

Nothing could be further from the truth. Enlightenment has nothing to do with spiritual experiences, just as not having spiritual experiences has nothing to do with not being enlightened. The Self exists beyond the field of experience or non-experience. However, as we deepen in the realization that there is nothing outside the Self, we are able to embrace all these emotions and experiences as part of the journey of life.

This is what the Buddhists call *equanimity*, and this is the mark of an enlightened person. Paradoxically, the less we chase after an exalted state of experience, and embrace each ordinary moment as it is, the more we can trust the flow of life, and deepen in the realization who we truly are.

Remember that hucha usually takes the form of resistance or attachment, which then translates into mental, emotional and physical symptoms. These attitudes derive from the fear that it is not safe to trust the universe, and creates the neurotic need to rigidly control all the details of our lives. We impede our ability to access the deeper wisdom that wishes to come through.

On the other hand, as we surrender to each of our life experiences, trusting in the natural goodness of life, it becomes easier to release this hucha. In so doing, life energies can move through us freely, and whatever kundalini overload we may be experiencing quickly dissipates.

A good exercise to practice in the midst of difficult life circumstances, including times when you are going through kundalini overload, is to ask yourself, "what am I afraid of?" Follow the trail of fears, layer by layer, like peeling an onion. There could be fears of losing control, fears of becoming physically incapacitated, fears of going crazy, fears of loss, fears of pain.

Underneath this there could be the fear of death. Let yourself go even deeper. If there is no death for the soul, even this fear eventually dissolves. Ultimately, we find that each fear we experience is ultimately a fear of change, based on our inability to trust the source of this change.

The Hopis warn us of a strong tide of change that is coming. The river is rising, they say, and we are trying to hold on to the riverbank, thinking we can remain safe. Let go, they tell us. You may not know where the river will take you, but the river knows. Trust the river.

As soon as we achieve this trust, we find that much of our fear dissolves, and as fear dissolves so does our resistance and need to control. The rivers of life can move through us freely for a purpose greater than our human minds can imagine.

Our rational mind is not designed for trust, nor for the ability to surrender to something unknown. But as the kundalini continues to flow, opening doorways between the worlds, we touch levels of the mind where this becomes possible. Unconditional peace and serenity flows in the midst of change, and we let go the final resistance offered by the personal ego before it joins the great ocean.

Once we know ourelves as the Self, all fear dissolves forever. "Sometimes we go about pitying ourselves," say the Ojibway Indians, "when all the time we are being carried on great big winds across the sky!"

CHAPTER 42
FOODS FOR HEALTH

As our bodies respond to the tides of change, we may find that our physical apetites vary from time to time. There may be times we are not hungry, and don't experience the need to eat. There are other times we want to eat voraciously. Foods that tasted good no longer appeal, and we develop cravings for other foods that we never liked before.

Many find that their cravings for heavy foods, including meat, begin to disappear, and they are attracted to fresh, raw organic foods, such as fruits, seeds and nuts. Others, who have been vegetarian or vegan for much of their lives, suddenly discover a craving for small quantities of meat. Some discover a need to cleanse the body, perhaps including a lengthy fast.

Ayurvedic medicine refers to three types of *doshas*, or temperaments, which correspond to different kinds of foods. These doshas are *vata, pitta* and *kapha*, which relate to a balance between the five elements of ether, air, fire, water and earth. They also correlate with the *gunas*, which are qualities of the mind.

There are three gunas, *sattva, rajas*, and *tamas*, which represent the mental equivalent of the doshas. They represent our journey into incarnation. Satva represents the subtlety of spirit, rajas represents energy and passion, and tamas represents the inertia of matter. When our doshas come into balance, and when the vibrational quality of our food becomes more refined, we enter into a sattvic state of mind, which can more easily perceive the truth of existence.

Our goal is not to remain in sattva however, but to bring his sattvic component into the rajasic and tamasic realms as well, preparing the body for higher downloads of spiritual force. As we align with this goal, a cellular wisdom takes over, and we find ourselves naturally drawn to what we need to eat in that moment.

There are some foods, however, that it would be well to avoid altogether. As our system purifies itself, it becomes more sensitive to toxic elements in our foods and environment. Most of the foods we find in the grocery store are heavily laden with pesticides or chemical agents. Many grains, fruits and vegetables are genetically modified, which often makes them incompatible with human DNA.

Many foods that served as staples for endless generations are no longer so healthy for us. Milk and milk products, along with commercially raised meat, are tainted with pesticides, hormones, antibiotics and steroids. Refined flours not only have their life force removed, but also contain toxic bleaching agents. White sugar is especially dangerous, while many sugar substitutes on the market are even worse.

GMO foods have been known to cause immune system disorders, food allergies, digestive problems and organ damage, while also adversely affecting our reproductive capabilities. Most corn, wheat and soybean crops available today are genetically modified, along with a high percentage of fruits and vegetables. Gluten sensitivities have also been linked to genetically modified grains.

It is not my intention to go into details here. There are many books and internet resources for those who wish to explore this further. However, you may find that as your body becomes increasingly purified, it starts to reject foods it may have enjoyed before. Some of this rejection could be in the form of allergies.

A good cleanse could be useful for detoxifying the body from accumulated poisons in the colon, liver, kidneys and other organs. Many have experienced not only the physical benefits of such a cleanse but also the mental clarity, emotional stability and spiritual illumination that follows.

Some people have even begun to explore what is known as pranic nutrition, or living on light. While teachers such as Jasmuheen have begun to popularize this in the West, there has been a long tradition of yogic practices in the East, including the practice of sun gazing, with the goal of refining the physical body so it can eventually merge with the light body.

There is a lineage in the Himalayas known as the *nath yogis,* whose goal was to create a mind of light, which could then be utilized to create a body of light, the linga sharir. There are many immortal masters who have evolved through this tradition. There are even stories of how the great master known as Jesus came to be associated with this lineage. Known in India as *Issa Nath,* he too attained the body of light, and remains to this day available for those who seek him.

The Tibetan tradition of taking the rainbow body echoes this understanding. There were established practices among the Egyptian, Chinese and Inka tradition for achieving this as well.

The science of evolutionary biology has also begun to examine this process. The German biologist, Fritz Albert-Popp coined the term *biophotons,* referring to a natural lumininiscence that can be measured within the mitochondria of cells. As we begin to explore and integrate the more subtle levels of our being, our aura expands out to the causal body, which allows the light of our primal Self to permeate the cells of our physical body.

The Inka paqos inform us that at the Sixth level of awareness our bodies literally begin to glow with light. Is this what the emergence of the next human species, *homo luminous,* is about?

CHAPTER 43
HOMO LUMINOUS

Sri Aurobindo speaks about four stages in the evolution of the human species. The first stage is the *animal human*, where our primary focus was the development of our natural insincts. We were highly attuned to the cycles and rhythms of nature, living in undifferentiated unity with the circle of life. The aboriginal tradition, and most indigenous cultures were at this stage. It was a primitive species, not in the sense of being inferior, but in terms of being primal.

The next stage is the *human human*. We are collectively at this stage now. Our task is to differentiate from the collective, develop a personal ego, and begin the process of individuation. This requires the development of reason as a tool for individuation, and also led to the development of the causal body as a permanent entity capable of storing our incarnational memories.

This is why the earlier Inka traditions, along with other aboriginal traditions, did not believe in a permanent soul. For them the soul was created at birth, borrowed from the apus, the living spirits of nature, and returned to the collective stream of nature when the body died.

With the human human species came the development of a more permanent, individual soul that was capable of imprinting the memories and feelings of our incarnational journey. It is this ability that distinguishes us from most other species on earth.

Unfortunately, our evolution is still incomplete. While we have learned to differentiate, we have not yet learned to individuate. Rather, we have rather set ourselves as separate and isolated from the rest of creation, needing to conquer, dominate, enslave and control others in order to feel safe and powerful. Because of the split inherent in our dualistic perspective of the world, the mind, heart, soul and spirit do not function harmoniously. The masculine and the feminine aspects of our being are not integrated.

The third stage of human evolution is about repairing this split in the fabric of humanity. Sri Aurobindo referred to this stage as the divine human, characterized by a return to unity. Rather than the undifferentiated unity of the animal human, this is an experience of conscious unity, where we intentionally co-create through the power of the Self. As we heal the split within our psyche, we join the masculine and feminine aspects of our being, and unify mind, heart, soul and spirit.

In this stage of human evolution, our relationship with the natural world changes radically. No longer do we need to enslave, dominate and conquer. We see ourselves as living cells of Gaia, intent on creating beauty and harmony for the entire web of life. Having integrated the laws of ayni, it becomes impossible to hurt or destroy another, for all creation becomes an aspect of my own extended self.

This is the stage of evolution that we preparing to enter now as a collective humanity. We are entering a phase of transition, referred to in different traditions as an *apocalypse, pralaya,* or *pachakuti,* where everything gets turned upside down, or more accurately, right side up.

There is a prayer in the Brihadaranyaka Upanishad, "Lead me from falsehood to truth, from darkness to light, from death to immortality." This represents the longing inherent in the human species for moving past the illusions of duality into the light of oneness, and to experience the deathlessness of soul as our larger identity.

Homo luminous is the Mayan term for this next race of humans. It literally means the luminous human. Sri Aurobindo referred to this race as the sun-eyed children of a marvelous dawn. This represents the third stage of human evolution.

But even this is not the final stage. He goes on to envision a fourth stage of humanity, perhaps a thousand years in our future, which he calls the *supramental being*. Here, the physical body also joins with heart, soul, mind and spirit in the experience of conscious unity. The physical body transforms into an immortal body of light. There are those in the sands of time who have achieved this feat on a personal level, but never has this been a biological possibility for collective humanity.

This becomes possible now through the entry of the highest level of mind, the *supramental*, into the density of matter. This is the work that Sri Aurobindo and the Mother had labored towards, and it was accomplished on February 29, 1956. The Mother described this event,

"I had a form of living gold, bigger than the universe, and I was facing a huge and massive golden door which separated the world from the Divine. As I looked at the door, I knew and willed, in a single movement of consciousness, that 'the time has come,' and lifting with both hand a mighty golden hammer I struck one blow, one single blow on the door, and the door was shattered to pieces. Then the supramental Light and Force and Consciousness rushed down upon earth in an uninterrupted flow."

Although imprinted now within the etheric body of the earth, the full revelation of this supramental force is still to come. Although the codes for a new biology have been seeded, they are still to manifest within the collective tree of life. The upcoming magnetic reversal could well be the mechanism for this collective manifestation. Exactly how this happens is up to us, and is also the subject of a companion volume, *Gaia Luminous*.

The divine human is emerging now on this earth with the first descent of supramental force. This will be the third stage of our evolution. Beyond this, perhaps awaiting a future cycle of magnetic reversal, there are those who will feel called to continue this supramental work within their own bodies, and within the body of the earth. And when it is complete we shall rise up from the ignorance of our foolish Age, strike one mighty blow upon the golden doors of destiny, and bring forth the fourth stage of supramental being into existence.

CHAPTER 44
THE NEW EARTH

The live in perilous times. We are seeing extreme climate changes, massive pollution, and irreversible destruction of species. We are experiencing social chaos, political unrest and economic uncertainties in an increasingly fragile world. Many fear that we may already have crossed the point of no return, spiraling rapidly into an extinction level event such as the one that wiped out the dinosaurs and most other species on our planet 66 million years ago.

Can we do anything to reverse this? As Einstein seems to have stated once, we cannot solve the problems of this age from the same level of consciousness that created them. So what then? It seems evident to me that the key lies in calling the supramental force deep into the heart of the earth, deep into the matrix of human consciousness, deep into all the social, economic and political structures we have created.

Sri Aurobindo said we would need to pass through a *supramental catastrophe* before the supramental descent could fully manifest in physical form. He is not referring to a 'super catastrophe' where everything gets wiped out. Rather, he is giving us a vision of hope. The supramental descent represents the entry of a unified field permeated with highly refined cosmic sami. As it moves through layers of collective hucha, it is capable of transmuting our collective darkness with the very minimum of destruction and suffering.

Likewise, the Andean prophecies speak of the pachakuti, an age where everthing gets turned upside down. These are not prophecies of doom, however, but rather a prelude to the return of the Inka, the illuminated ones. They speak of repairing the 'tear in the fabric of time', which means stepping outside the matrix of linear time, exploring our full human potential, and then coming back to heal the world.

Part of this healing involves changing our myth of Creation. The indigenous people of the world were never kicked out from the Garden of Eden. They have always been able to talk with the trees, listen to the wind, and commune with the land. Eve, rather than taking the blame for all the suffering of the earth, must now be seen as the face of the Great Mother. We must rediscover our relationship with Pachamama, and build the tree of life. It is only through this that we can re-enter the garden.

We are in a time of transition. People around the world are waking up to find their balance. We are learning about ayni and right action, discovering that we are not separate from the earth. Perhaps this is a reflection of a planetary initiation that Mother Earth herself is undergoing.

The Inka prophecy states that all of us will achieve the Fifth Level simultaneously. This is similar to the assertion of Sri Aurobindo and the Mother that the divine human will emerge naturally from within the current human species, just as the butterfly emerges from within a caterpillar. It is a biological transformation, an evolutionary leap.

Evolutionary leaps and magnetic reversals go together. Our current phase of magnetic reversal has been underway for the past two hundred years or more. The magnetic field strength is weakening at an exponential rate, and we are being prepared for the final phase of reversal, which in past ages has often been sudden and dramatic. The path of the magnetic poles across the earth has also been shifting steadily. It is likely that the reversal itself, with all the corresponding upheavals in consciousness, could take place very shortly.

This reversal would trigger immense electromagnetic impulses around the planet, releasing fiery kundalini energies within the earth, and within the collective planes of human consicousness. Like a phoenix plunging into the flames and rising renewed from the ashes, there is the potential for a complete reset of the human matrix.

The supramental transformation is inevitable, says Sri Aurobindo, but the transition may be somewhat challenging. Our job now is to attune with the field of Gaia, bring the supramental force inside ourselves, and to consciously speed up and direct the forces of evolution.

What is the nature of this supramental force? Unlike other levels of the mind, which function as windows into various aspects of reality, the supermind has a light of its own. Imbued with the power of truth consciousness it cannot help but disperse ignorance wherever it is directed. As it shines upon the fractured matrix of a dualistic age, it instantly reveals the consciousness of unity that underlies everything. As it shines upon human structures built on ignorance, greed, aggression and fear, they instantly collapse.

It's like my dream of confronting the terrifying monster, which suddenly became a terrified little turkey. When seen in the light of truth consciousness, all the frightening global issues we currently face can be very quickly transmuted. The asuric forces of falsehood, death, darkness and fear, which have ravaged the earth during this past world age, can be absorbed back into the undifferentiated light of the Great Mother.

If we are to shine this light, however, we must first realize ourselves as this light. As we open the doorway between worlds, this light begins to pour in as waves of intuitions and revelations, insights and ecstasies, power and intent, growing in intensity until it becomes a single, uninterrupted flow. Knowledge becomes clear, senses become subtle, the heart opens to all worlds of creation, and the will becomes a golden hammer in the forges of destiny.

David Hawkins describes a logarithmic scale of consciousness, which ranges from total separation at zero to absolute unity at one thousand. It describes human values, attitudes and emotions in terms of where they would be placed on this scale.

Interestingly, the higher you are on this scale, the more direct influence you have on the collective consciousness of humanity.

Even a few people vibrating at the upper end of this scale would be enough to transform this earth. These would be the fifth and sixth degree initiates, or those who have managed to bring the supramental force into their bodies.

The supramental force is a power of truth consciousness, in the light of which all ignorance instantly falls away. But to shine this light requires that there be no shadows remaining within our own psyche, no more resistance to the flow of the divine. It requires a unification of heart, mind and will.

It is not an ordinary work, and requires much dedication, time and effort. Gaia does not require masses of people to accomplish this. But She does require those select few who are willing to release their personal agendas, become guardians for a world beyond the 'matrix', and take their place as forerunners in the Age of Light:

I saw the Omnipotent's flaming pioneers

Over the heavenly verge which turns towards life

Come crowding down the amber stairs of birth

Forerunners of a divine multitude.

Out of the paths of the morning star they came

Into the little room of mortal life.

I saw them cross the twilight of an age

The sun-eyed children of a marvellous dawn

Great creators with wide brows of calm

The massive barrier-breakers of the world

And wrestlers with destiny in her lists of will

The labourers in the quarries of the gods

The messengers of the Incommunicable

The architects of Immortality.

Sri Aurobindo, Savitri

BIBLIOGRAPHY

Aurobindo, Sri. *The Life Divine*. Sri Aurobindo Ashram Trust

Aurobindo, Sri. *The Supramental Manifestation upon Earth*. Sri Aurobindo Ashram Trust, 1995.

Felix, Robert W. *Magnetic Reversals and Evoluionary Leaps: The True Origin of Species*. Bellevue: Sugarhouse Publishing, 2009.

Jasmuheen, *Living on Light: A Source of Nutrition for the New Millenium*. Koha Publishing, 1997.

Jenkins, Elizabeth. *Return of the Inka: A Journey of Initiation and Prophecies for 2012*. Pu'umuka'a Press, 2009.

Jenkins, Elizabeth. *The Fourth Level: Nature Wisdom. Teachings of the Inka*. Create Space, 2013.

Polich, Judith Bluestone. *Return of the Children of Light: Incan and Mayan Prophecies for a New World*. Bear & Co., 2001.

Swartz, James. *How to Attain Enlightenment: The Vision of Nonduality*. Sentient Publications, 2010.

Swartz, James. *The Yoga of the Three Energies*. Sentient Publications, 2017.

Satprem. *Sri Aurobindo and the Adventure of Consciousness*. Mira Aditi Center, 2008.

Satprem. *On the Way to Supermanhood*. Mira Aditi Center, 2002.

Van Vrekehem, Georges. *Beyond Human: The Life and Work of Sri Aurobindo and the Mother*. Rupa & Co, 1997.

Wilcox, Joan Parisi. *Masters of the Living Energy: The Mystical World of the Q'ero of Peru*. Inner Traditions, 2004.

Windrider, Kiara. *Gaia Luminous: Emergence of the New Earth*. Kima Books: Cape Town, 2017.

Windrider, Kiara. *Ilahinoor: Awakening the Divine Human*. Notion Press: Chennai, 2017.

Windrider, Kiara. *Issa, Son of the Sun*

GLOSSARY OF QUECHUA TERMS

Amaru – anaconda, snake-like living energy

Atiy – self-confidence

Ayni – law of reciprocity

Ayllu – close family

Chaki – foot centers

Chakuy – bridge

Chumpi – energy belts

Chumpi away – weaving the belts

Despacho - ceremony

Hampi – healing, medicine

Hampi munay muyu – healing circle of love

Hanaq pacha – upper world

Hoqari kallpachi – upward healing energy

Hucha – blocked or heavy energy

Hucha mikhuy – practice of digesting hucha

Inka - illumined

Inka muyu – seed of light

Kausay – universal life energy

Kausay pacha – the universe

Kanay – recovering memory of your true self

Karu ayllu pacha – distant family

Kay pacha – middle world

Khuya – stone of power

Kunka – throat

Glossary of Quechua terms

Kurku – spine

Llankay – action energy

Lloqe - left

Maki – hand centers

Micha or mesa – medicine bundle

Mikhuy – to digest

Munay – heart energy

Munay muyu – circle of love

Nawi - the eye of each energy center

Nawi kichay – energizing the channels

Naupa pacha – the past

Pacha – world

Pachakuti – turning upside down, time of transition

Pachamama – mother earth, cosmic mother

Pana - right

Paqo – shaman or mystic

Pichay – sweeping, downward healing energy

Pichay mikhuy – practice for sweeping out hucha

Popqo – energy bubble or luminous egg

Poqpo taqe – sharing energy through the bubble

Puyju – fontanelle

Qanchis - seven

Qanchis samin seqe – seven sharings

Qanchis Seqe – the seven cords

Qaya pacha – the future

Qinse pacha seqe – channel of concentrated light

Qosqo – spiritual stomach located at navel

Rhapy – the root of each energy center

Rimay – power to express your authentic self

Salka – wildness, undomesticated energy

Sami – flowing aspect of kausay, experienced in the body as lightness of heart

Samin chakuy – bridge connecting sky to earth

Saywa – column of energy

Saywa chakuy – bridge connecting earth to sky

Saywa taqe – sharing column of refined energy

Seqe – cord or leyline connecting places, people or things

Siki – root

Sonqo - heart

Soqtantin – six

Taqe – sharing refined energy

Taripay pacha – age of meeting ourselves again

Tarpuy – to plant

Tusuy – quality of action

Ukhu pacha – lower world

Uma – crown

Wachay – ancestral lineage

Wanuy – dying

Wasi – poqpo plus physical body

Willka – black light

Willka muyu – seed of black light

Wiracocha – cosmic father

Yachay – thinking energy

INDEX

ABOUT THE AUTHOR

Kiara Windrider spent much of his early life traveling and practicing various spiritual traditions in India. A lifelong interest in environmental awareness, peace making, and social justice led to a dual degree in Peace studies and International Development through Bethel College, North Newton, Kansas.

Later, he completed a graduate program in Transpersonal Counseling Psychology through JFK University in Orinda, California, and worked for many years at an alternative psychiatric center called Pocket Ranch Institute, which specialized in healing emotional trauma and facilitating spiritual emergence. He received a psychotherapy license (MFT) from the State of California in 1998. He has also trained in various forms of bodywork, breathwork, hypnotherapy, and shamanic healing.

Kiara is an avid science researcher, exploring connections between galactic cycles, climate change, ancient history, quantum physics, human behavior and spiritual awakening. As an outcome of this extensive research he has come to the firm conviction that we stand collectively at the brink of a quantum evolutionary leap beyond our wildest dreams.

He is currently focused on planetary healing using a system of anchoring divine light known as Ilahinoor. He also teaches Inka shamanic practices, into which he was initiated by Juan Nunez del Prado and Ivan Nunez del Prado. Kiara has worked with Egyptian, Huna and Sufi traditions, and is also rooted in Integral Yoga and the Advaita traditions of India.

He offers workshops and retreats worldwide for awakening to our infinite potential. His greatest wish is to live fully in the wonder of each moment, and to help awaken this beautiful planet to its luminous destiny.

Kiara is the author of Doorway to Eternity: A Guide to Planetary Ascension, Deeksha: Fire from Heaven, Journey into Forever: Surfing 2012 and Beyond, Year Zero: Time of the Great Shift, Ilahinoor: Awakening the Divine Human, Gaia Luminous: Emergence of the New Earth, and Issa: Son of the Sun.

Please check out his website, Kiarawindrider.net.

Suggestions and comments are always welcome, and may be addressed to kiarawindrider@gmail.com.